It's Showtime!

A Beginner's Guide to Showing Draft Horses

By
Robert A. Mischka

Heart Prairie Press
Whitewater, Wisconsin

Published by
Mischka Farm
N8246 Esterly Road
Whitewater WI 53190
(414) 473 5595

Publisher's Cataloging in Publication Data
>   Mischka, Robert A., 1934 -
>   It's Showtime: a beginner's guide to showing draft
>   horses / by Robert A. Mischka. -- 1st ed.
>   p. cm.
>   ISBN: 1-882199-04-9
>
>   1. Horses--Showing--United States. 2. Draft horses. 3.
>   Show horses. I. Title.

SF295.M57 1998   798.2
                                  QB197-41602

Special thanks to Robert Kline, Extension Horse Specialist at the Ohio State University, for permission to use drawings from the 4-H Circular *Draft Horse* authored by Kristin Myers.

Front Cover: Randy Robinson trots the 3 yr-old Clydesdale stallion, Muirton Sceptre, at the 1979 National Clydesdale show in Milwaukee with the judge, Mr. Bill Brass, looking on.

Back Cover: Robert Mischka showing the gelding, Willy, in the Men's Cart class at the 1987 Michigan Great Lakes International show. Photo by Melissa.

Endpapers: Joe Mischka is driving two Mischka Farm mares, Mi Karla and Mi Brunhilda. Riding with Joe is his brother, Justin. The homemade wagon box is mounted on an antique running gear with rebuilt wheels.

Preface

Each year there are new people "getting into draft horses." This usually means that someone, often with a riding horse background, decides to purchase a draft horse for recreational purposes. A year or two later they may decide to show their draft horse in halter at the local county fair or state fair, especially if they were previously involved in showing their riding horses. This often leads to the decision to show their horse (or horses) in harness, starting with a single horse in a cart. The progression is very predictable, as showing in cart leads to showing pairs (and more) hooked to a wagon. And if showing at local shows is successful and fun the progression to larger regional or national shows soon follows.

Our family went through this progression. Each of our five boys showed riding horses, both under saddle and in harness. As the boys grew up and left home Mary and I were left with a horsebarn and indoor arena, and we bought a Percheron filly. A year later we bred the mare and she gave us the first of six consecutive fillies. When we bred these fillies they also gave us fillies, and we soon had a large herd of registered Percherons. We showed our mares, first in halter and then in harness. This was the time (the early 1980s) when many of the larger shows were adding hitch classes for registered mares. Our mares were "hitchy" and did very well in those classes.

We found that showing draft horses was, in many ways, quite different from showing light horses. This book should help the draft horse newcomer avoid some mistakes when showing their horses and thereby have a safer and more enjoyable experience.

As with most things involving horses there are usually many different ways to do something, and often there is no single "right way." Many professional draft horsemen and "old-time" draft horse people have developed their own unique ways to fit and show their horses. Each of these professionals and/or "old-timers" knows more about showing draft horses than I do, but they are unlikely to sit down and write a book about their experiences and methods. As you embark on this adventure of showing draft horses please talk and listen to the other exhibitors at a show. Horse people love to talk about their horses, and draft horse people are usually very generous with their help and advice. Search out someone who appears to treat their animals well, and who is successful, and ask their advice when you have a problem. You will make friends and learn something.

Robert Mischka
February, 1998

Table of Contents

Table of Contents (continued)

Dedication

To Mary — my wife, best friend, and companion for 45 wonderful years. Thanks for the memories.

Introduction

Showing draft horses can take many different forms, from walking behind a plow at a local field day to driving six matched geldings at the National Horse Show. Between these two extremes we have horse-pulls, parades of all sizes and types, and local and regional shows. Each of these activities involves the presentation of draft horses to the general public — that is, "showing draft horses". Although the great majority of this book will deal with what is conventionally meant by showing (the presentation of horses at halter and in harness at a horse show) it is important, at the outset, to understand that most of the principles regarding the selection, conditioning, training, grooming, and presentation of draft horses apply to all activities where we bring out our horses and show them to the public.

People showing draft horses can be generally divided into two groups: professionals who show horses as a business and amateurs who show horses as a hobby. The professionals are usually employees who fit and show horses full-time. They are often from a family that has raised and shown draft horses for many generations. Their employers are showing a hitch for public relations purposes or are showing their horses at halter to advertise their farm and/or breeding program. These professionals know more about showing draft horses than I will ever know. This book is written for the other group — the people who want to show their draft horses as a hobby.

Showing draft horses can and should be fun. If it isn't fun, why do it? The people attracted to draft horses, both in the ring and outside it, are generally down-to-earth sensible types — the kind of people you might pick out of a group for friends. Draft horse showing is usually a family activity, with the owner or a member of the owner's family doing the showing. This often results in reduced tension and less pressure than is common at light horse shows.

We are fortunate in this part of the world in that most of us have some free time, and we use some of this free time for recreation. Showing draft horses often involves the entire family, with most shows in the summer months when the children are out of school. In this age of television and splintered families a recreational activity that tends to bring and keep families together is surely a good thing.

Raising and keeping draft horses is expensive. As soon as you decide to take your draft horses away from home — to show them — these expenses increase dramatically. The expenses involved in showing draft horses fall somewhere between the cost of golf and yachting.

Showing draft horses also involves a great deal of hard work. That's why it's important that it also be fun. There's no point in doing the work unless you enjoy it. The enjoyment you get from showing should make you forget the work involved.

We enjoyed showing our draft horses, and hope that the tips you will find in this book will help make it an enjoyable experience for you.

Alan Schneckloth drives a team of his father's Belgians at the 1980 Wisconsin State Fair. Alan is now the lead driver for the Budweiser hitch based in St. Louis.

Chapter One
Conformation and Unsoundness

GENERAL

Before we get into the subject of showing it will be helpful to spend a little time looking at the other side of the coin — the judging process.

If you have many horses at your place and need to select which ones to show you'll have to do some judging yourself to help decide which ones to to take and which to leave. It is more likely, however, that as a newcomer to draft horses you have only a few animals and there are no choices involved — you simply take the horses you have. But even then you will want to know something of how the judging works so you will better understand why your animals are placed where they are in the class. The judge will seldom volunteer any reasons for his placings.

If you are going to show you have to learn about judging.

Since we will be using the names of the various parts of the horse throughout this Chapter we'd better start by showing where these parts are.

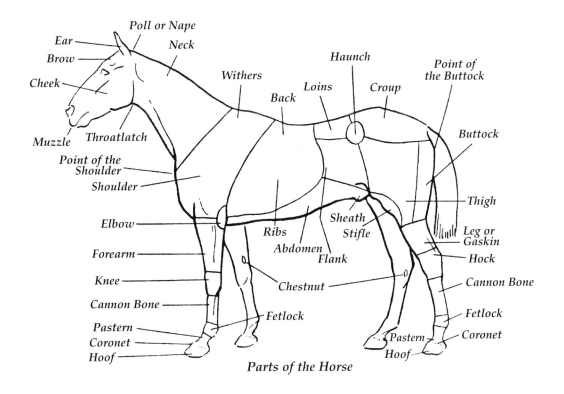

Parts of the Horse

The perfect horse does not exist. Do not be discouraged if your horse does not possess all the desirable characteristics described in the following paragraphs.

Some of the characteristics described below will be hard for the newcomer to distinguish. Some are subtle, and many are described in rather vague terms such as good, long, short, graceful, etc. It is normal for the newcomer to have difficulty in understanding exactly what is meant by the following descriptions. People who are good at judging horses have been at it for many years, and many do it during most of their waking hours. It takes time and practice to become a proficient judge of horses.

There is no easy short-cut to becoming a good judge of horses.

DESIRABLE CONFORMATION AND CONFORMATION FAULTS

The head should be in proportion to the rest of the body. A slightly Roman nose is appropriate on the Clyde and Shire, but not on the Belgian or Percheron. The eyes should large, bright, and set wide apart. Blindness is an unsoundness, and should be checked by moving your hand in front of the eye. A slight arch between the eyes is desirable, as is a wide muzzle with large nostrils. The ears should be set at the top of the head and they should be active. There should be no missing front teeth, and these teeth should meet properly with no under or over-bite.

The neck should be long and graceful with a straight line on the bottom and a slight crest on the top. Stallions should have more crest than mares or geldings. Mares with a pronounced crest will be penalized in the showring. The throatlatch should be clean and slender, not bunched up and meaty.

The angle of the shoulder should be well sloped at a 45° angle. This will allow the horse to get his head up and will increase his action at the trot. A more vertical angle will result in a lower head-set.

The back should be short and fairly level. The withers should be strong and pronounced. There should be good

The Reserve Champion Jr Mare at the Belgian Championship II show was Remlap Constance Edie Johne shown by Beth Graham.

width and depth to the body, with the ribs well-sprung. The hind-quarters (croup, buttock, and thigh) should be round, strong, and well-muscled. The croup should be flat, fairly level, and not fall off sharply. The tail should be set high on the croup.

The forearm should be longer than the cannon on the front leg. The knee should be large, squarish, and flat when viewed from the front. The cannon bones should be flat and sharply defined. There should be no splints on the back of the cannon where they might interfere with the tendons.

The most important part of any horse, including the draft horse, is its legs — their shape, location, and set. The following drawings illustrate the ideal front leg shape and position, along with the many undesirable variations that may occur.

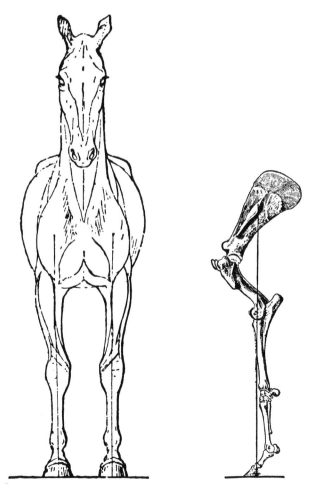

The correct front leg from the front and side. Note the slope and length of the pastern.

Base-narrow or splay-footed

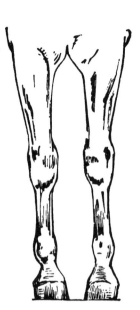

Toe-narrow or pigeon-toed

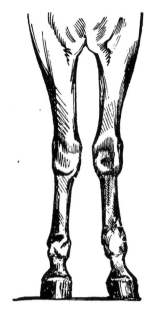

Knock-kneed

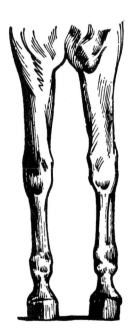

Bow-kneed

Too close at the ground

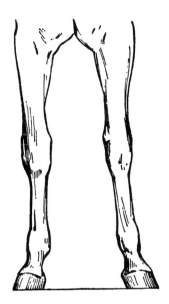

Too wide at the ground

Various types of front legs when viewed from the front

Knee-sprung or over-on-the-knees   *Calf-kneed*   *Too straight in Pastern*

Various types of front legs when viewed from the side.

The pasterns are very important. They absorb the shock when the foot hits the ground, especially at the trot and canter. The pasterns should be long, smooth, and have a nice 45° to 50° slope. Pasterns that are short and steep will eventually cause lameness. The pastern and ankle joint should be trim with no trace of swelling or puffiness.

The hock is also very important on a draft horse. Swelling in the hock area (filled hocks) is very common with draft horses, and is a serious fault which is not always easy for the newcomer to see. To make sure there is no swelling you may have to feel or squeeze the hock to check for puffiness. Bony protrusions in the hock area, called a bone spavin, are considered an unsoundness for they will probably cause lameness. A curb is a swelling due to a strain of the ligament below the hock. It may go away with rest, but is an unsoundness when you see it. A hock is capped when it has a loose swelling on the back point. In summary the hock should be clean, hard, and broad, and the point at the back should be prominent. There should be no fleshiness or puffiness of any kind in the hock area.

It is important that the hock be hard and flat, with no swelling or puffiness.

The following drawings illustrate the proper position and shape of the hind leg.

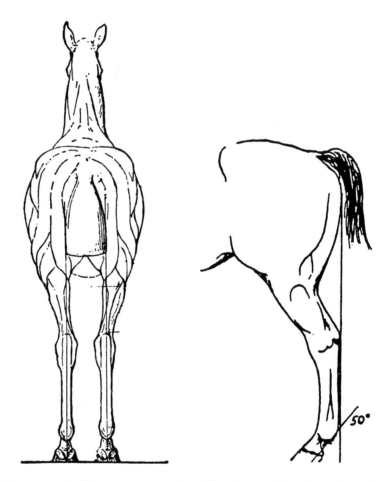

The correct hind leg. Note that a plumb line dropped from the point of the buttock will touch the back of the hock and run down parallel to the cannon bone.

Today most show horses are shod with their hind feet turned out. This is done to move their hocks closer together than is shown in the drawing above. I will talk more about this in Chapter Seven on Shoeing. The main thing is that the rear cannon bones are parallel to each other, regardless of how close they are to one another.

The most common fault in the hind leg of a draft horse is having too much curve — a condition which is called sickle-hocked or crooked-legged. Three main faults of the hind leg are illustrated below.

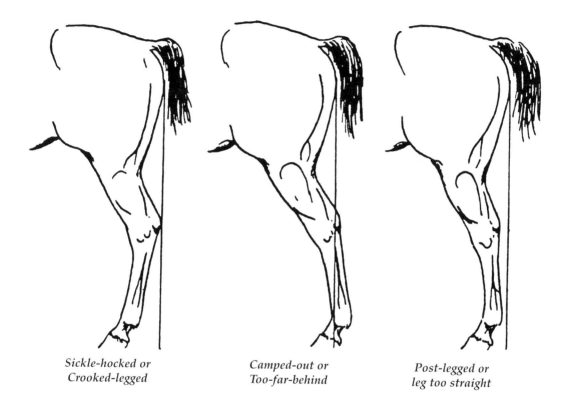

Sickle-hocked or Crooked-legged

Camped-out or Too-far-behind

Post-legged or leg too straight

The hoof should have a large, round hoof head; a strong, dense wall; and a wide heel. Contracted heels are a fault that will lead to lameness or other problems.

A normal heel on the left compared to a contracted heel on the right.

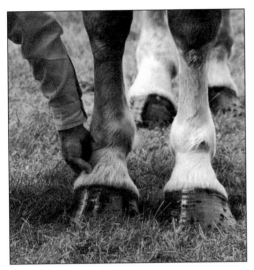

Checking for sidebones.

When you see the judge bend down and push on the back of the front feet, behind the heel of the hoof, he is checking for **sidebones**. On both sides of hoof, behind the coffin bone, there is a large, flat cartilage called the lateral cartilage. It forms a yielding and elastic wall to the sensitive structures within the foot.

This lateral cartilage gradually becomes ossified (turns to bone) as the horse grows older. When this change occurs prematurely it is called a sidebone. You will hear people say things like "a little hard on the corners" to describe this condition. It seldom occurs on horses younger than 3 years old, and usually occurs on the front feet where the horse carries most of his weight.

To check for sidebones you should face the rear of the horse, bend down, and wrap your hand around the horse's ankle. With your thumb and finger-tips toward the back of the hoof you will push on the area in front of the bulb of the heel. It should feel soft and bend inward when you push on it. If it is rigid and does not flex, you probably have a sidebone. Be sure that any hardness you feel is not some sort of scabbing or hardening due to a recent injury, and check both sides of the foot. A severe case of sidebones is easy to see, without feeling the hoof, as the area is enlarged and often hairless.

The lateral cartilage will ossify due to excessive concussion when other defects occur such as steep shoulders, short pasterns, and contracted heels. Other causes are improper shoeing (nails too far back); injuries such as stepping on the back of the front heel with the

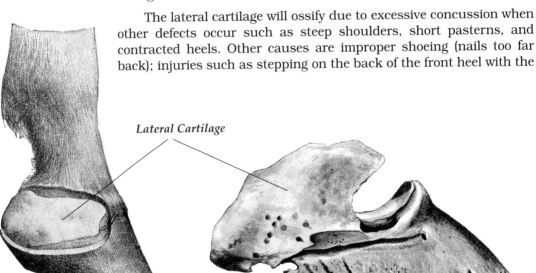

Lateral Cartilage

The lateral cartilage is the large area above.

Another view of the lateral cartilage showing that it really is quite a large structure.

back feet or dropping the end of a wagon pole on the back of the foot; and laminitis.

Sidebones are an unsoundness because the hoof has lost some of its elastic properties and lameness may eventually result. This was a bigger problem years ago, when draft horses delivered the goods in the cities and pounded the pavement all day, all week long. This seldom happens today, but sidebones are still considered a serious problem, especially by older horsemen. Some people believe sidebones to be hereditary, but most now feel that the conditions

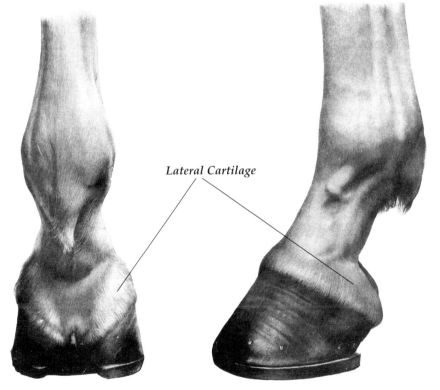

Lateral Cartilage

Sidebones are a controversial and often misunderstood fault when judging draft horses.

The lateral cartilage (which, when ossified is called a sidebone) is quite a large area at the side and back of the foot, above the coronet.

which might contribute to sidebones (narrow heels or steep pasterns) are hereditary, not the sidebones themselves. This is a rather picky distinction. You can still say that certain bloodlines have a predisposition for sidebones.

The 1936 booklet *How to Select Percherons* states that "some horses are penalized in the showring because of sidebones, and others under another judge are not." The booklet goes on to say that less than half of the 100 best judges "objected seriously to small sidebones". This situation is no different today, some 60 years later.

Some judges consider sidebones to be a fatal flaw and horses with this condition automatically go to the bottom of the class. Other judges don't even bother to check for them. And still others who **do** check are not sure what they're looking for, and will call something a sidebone when it is not.

Lameness is a fatal flaw in the showring and horses that are lame must be excused or placed at the bottom of the class.

WAY OF GOING

First and foremost, the horse must not be lame. Any indication of lameness, regardless of the reason, is cause for dismissal from the ring or being placed at the bottom of the class. Lameness is usually the result of pain. Front leg lameness usually is indicated by a bobbing of the head, with the head going up when the painful leg hits the ground. Rear leg lameness is indicated when one rear quarter drops lower at the trot. The side which drops lower is the lame side.

The normal gait for the draft horse is the walk. It is important that it be a good walker. The head should be carried high and the stride should be regular. The feet should be lifted clear of the ground and placed down evenly and in a straight line, as if in deliberation. Viewed from the back, the hock action should be free and straight.

At the trot the the horse should lift its knees and hocks with style and purpose. When viewed from the back the horse should show you the bottom of each hoof as he trots away from you.

The horse should cover some ground at both the walk and trot. Horses that take lots of steps but don't seem to get anywhere are called "blanket trampers."

Defects in a horse's way of going include winging or paddling when the front foot swings out before coming back to the ground. This is a fault frequently found in draft horses, especially when they are shod with an

The celebrated Belgian mare, E.J.G. Barb, owned by John Leask and shown here by Don Lowes, was the dominant Belgian mare in the 1990's.

oversize foot and heavy shoe. It is easy to see when watching the horse trot while standing in front of it. Forging is when the hind foot strikes the underside of the front foot at a trot. Interfering is when the right foot hits the left leg (or vice versa) during a stride. Another defect is when a horse places its front feet in the same track. This is called rope walking.

Unsoundness of wind (roarers) is difficult to detect in a halter class, but is quite obvious in a performance (hitch) class. If you suspect a wind problem you should have the horse trot away and back again several times at a lively pace and then listen to him breathe.

BLEMISHES VS. UNSOUNDNESS

A blemish is a defect or mark on a horse that does not interfere with its usefulness. An example would be a wire cut on the leg that left a scar but is now healed, with no resultant swelling or interior damage. Horses are frequently banged up when being transported to the show. These superficial injuries are blemishes. A slightly capped hock or elbow which does not interfere with the horse's movement would be a blemish. Small splints on the side of the cannon can be considered blemishes as they are no problem for the horse, and often will disappear as the horse gets older.

Blemishes, as contrasted with unsoundnesses, are not important and should be ignored when judging.

Rick Riemer driving a pair of Percheron geldings owned by Harold Schumacher at the 1991 Britt (Iowa) show.

Chapter Two
Ideal Breed Type

After you have evaluated the animals being judged for unsoundness and for conformation faults you are left to deal with the concept of breed type. Breed type is the overall appearance of the horse — the characteristics that make the various breeds look different from each other.

Draft Horse judging for breed type involves comparing the subjective qualities of utility and beauty found in a particular horse to these same qualities found in another horse. In addition to this direct comparison there is an implied comparison of the horse being judged to a standard or ideal in the "mind's eye" of the judge. In this second chapter we will talk about the somewhat elusive concept of **Ideal Breed Type** — the ideal horse in the judge's mind.

There is very little difference, except for color, between the modern Belgian and Percheron horse in North America.

When you first think about Ideal Breed Type it is natural to turn to the various breed Associations and ask them for their guidelines. Alas, you will find that the Associations cannot tell you what their ideal horse is because there is no agreement within their membership on what such an Ideal Breed Type would be. Breed type is an ever-changing concept. What is fashionable today is different from what was fashionable 30 years ago. This is true of literally everything, from morals to clothes to cars, and it is also true of draft horses.

As a practical matter we tend to get around this problem by accepting the idea that the animals which are placed at the top of the class in today's shows are, by definition, today's Ideal Breed Type. When looking at the situation from one week to the next, or even from one year to the next, this seems to work out alright. But when you look at Ideal Breed Type over a slightly longer period of time you will see significant changes in the type of horse that is selected as ideal.

In just the past 30 years there has been a dramatic change in all the major breeds in North America. This has been especially true for

Dale House showing House's Ted Farceur, the most celebrated Belgian Stallion in 1979-80.

the Belgian breed. Today's winning Belgian horses are taller, leggier, lighter-boned, higher-stepping, more refined about the head, and generally more stylish than those that were being shown just a few years ago. Except for color (the Belgian is now almost always a red sorrel with white mane, tail and stripe) the top Belgian horses of today are the same as the top Percherons. Most judges would find it difficult to pick out a sorrel Percheron in a class of Belgians.

Eighty years ago the winning Belgian and Percheron horses stood on back legs set out on the corners, with plenty of space between the back legs. Now they all stand close behind, like the Clyde, with hocks almost touching — as if a strong wind might blow them over.

The Peter Stone Company is in the business of making model horses. Recently they made a model of a Percheron Stallion patterned after the Grand Champion at the 1995 Michigan Great Lakes International, M.G.'s Prince. They offer this same model in several different colors — black and dapple grey as Percherons and blond and red sorrel as a Belgian. They apparently believe that there is very little difference between the Percherons and Belgians, except for color.

You will hear people decry today's trend toward a lighter, less drafty, leggier draft horse, especially in the Percheron and Belgian breeds. This complaint is often expressed by breeders who continue to breed the shorter, heavier horse either out of their conviction of the superiority of that type or because they own the chunkier type and it takes time to change. These breeders have a problem selling their horses at top prices.

You will often hear the complaint made that the "Modern type" has become a "coach horse", and is no longer a draft horse.

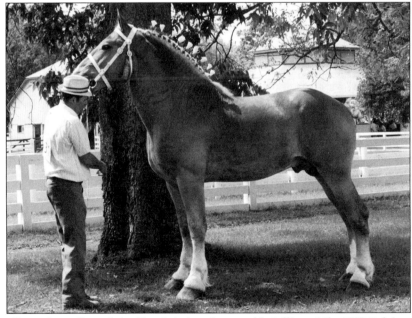

Green Acres Congolaise Jim, 1st place 3 year-old stallion at the 1992 Belgian Championship II Show.

Jay Farceur, one of the most noted Belgian stallions in North America this Century. Here he is shown after winning the 1938 International Live Stock Exposition.

Abernathy photo provided by Jim Richendollar.

Maple Creek Mack, a 19 hand 7 year-old Belgian stallion owned by Country Pride Belgians. Contrast this horse with Jay Farceur shown above in conformation and the refinement about the head.

Laet, foaled in 1916, one of the most celebrated Percheron stallions of all time. He is shown here as a five year-old.

Abernathy photo provided by Jim Richendollar.

The 2 year-old Belgian filly, Taylor Creek Stric-O-Luck, 1st out of 47 in her class at the 1992 Belgian Championship Show, being shown by Bob Whisman.

Northwest Glenords Shea, Grand Champion Clyde stallion at the 1993 Michigan International for Live Oak Plantation.

This is followed by a lament to the effect that the breed is being ruined.

The 1914 book *Productive Horse Husbandry* by Carl W. Gay tells that in the 19th Century the primary use for Percheron horses was to pull stage coaches. To meet this need they developed a coach horse which could pull relatively light loads over long distances at high speeds. This type of Percheron was called a diligence horse, and it *looks very similar to the modern Percheron of today.*

When the railroads came into prominence in the late 1800s they eliminated the stage coach, and Percheron breeders saw a need for heavier, stronger horses for agricultural use (to replace the oxen then being used) and for commercial freight hauling in the rapidly growing cities. To meet this need they developed the Percheron of the early 20th Century — a horse that could pull heavier loads over shorter distances at slower speeds.

In the past 75 years the Percheron horse in North America has changed from a coach horse to a farm/dray horse and then back to a coach horse.

Now, as the 20th Century comes to a close we find that there is little demand for the Percheron in agriculture or trucking and it is being "modernized" back to a coach horse for leisure-time activities. Times do change, and horses change with the times. What goes around comes around. And it is this constant change that makes the Breed Associations resist the pressure to promulgate an Ideal Breed Type. It gets to be a very politically charged discussion.

If you ask the Percheron Association for some guidelines on Ideal Breed Type they will send you a little booklet called *How to Select Percherons.* This booklet was written in 1936, and the horses pictured in this booklet (1900 to 1930) are generally stockier, with more bone and with less leg than is fashionable now. They stand square on the corners in back, rather than with their cannons together as they do now. Few of these horses would stand at the top of their class today.

The Percheron Association realized that this booklet was out of date so they revised it in 1986 to include pictures of four horses that were winning in 1984. The difference in appearance between these four and the other (earlier) horses is easy to see. The reader is left to decide for himself which group of horses is the Ideal Breed Type, but he knows that the horses that are winning in the showring today are more like the 1984 horses than the 1930 horses. This booklet is a good illustration of how breed type changes over time.

Another vivid illustration of the changes in the Percheron breed during the past 30 years can be found by picking up any recent copy of their January edition of Percheron News. These magazines usually contain an article by Benno Selcke in which he shows pictures of the top Percherons in France today. The French Percheron has changed very little in the recent past. If anything it has gotten a little more stocky since most French Percherons are raised for the meat trade. A quick look at these French horses and a comparison to the American horses depicted in the ads throughout the rest of the magazine will show you how much the American horse has changed. The French Percheron appears to be a different breed entirely.

The fact that the North American Percheron and Belgian horses are so different now from their ancestors in Europe has pretty much stopped the export trade from Europe to America. There are a limited number of horses now going the other way, from North America to Europe.

The Percheron folks do not, at present, have a good answer to this question, but they recognize it as a problem and are working on a solution. The Percheron Association established a committee at their October 1996 Annual Meeting to study the question of Ideal Breed Type. It will be interesting to see how this Committee approaches and deals with this problem. I am unaware of any effort to establish or define breed type for the Belgian horse in North America.

> The Percheron Association has formed a committee to tackle the problem of Ideal Breed Type.

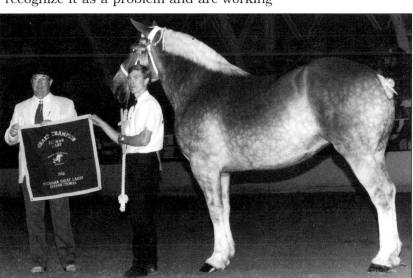

Orndordorff's Supreme Unity, Grand Champion Brood Mare at the major shows in 1992, shown by Corbly Orndorff at the 1992 Michigan International. Jack Cunningham, then Secretary of the Belgian Corporation, is presenting the banner.

Today's Clydesdale horse has undoubtedly been influenced by what we can call "The Budweiser Horse". There is a steady demand for a tall, bay horse for Budweiser's many hitches and theme parks — a fact which is not lost on Clyde breeders. Today's Clydes tend to be leggy bays, with white markings, which bear little resemblance to the Clyde that worked in farms fifty years ago.

For the Clydesdale and Shire breeders there is a little booklet called *A Beginner's Guide to Basic Conformation and Judging of Clydesdales* written by Marion Young which can be obtained from the Clydesdale Breeders Association. The information in Marion's booklet is helpful in learning about breed type and conformation faults in all draft breeds, not just Clydes and Shires.

Changes in the Suffolk breed are slow to develop due to the smaller number of animals involved. Today's Suffolk owners do not show their animals, and they generally seem content with keeping the breed as it has been.

When we first got into draft horses after showing riding horses for many years I found it difficult to tell the difference between one Percheron and another. These subjective differences, and many of

Henry Junkans drives the Argonaut Farm Shire six at the 1991 Britt Show. Riding with Hank is Randy Riemer. This hitch was a "crowd's favorite" wherever it was shown.

the structural ones, eluded me. It was like looking at a herd of Holstein cows — but worse — for the cows at least had differently shaped spots. I knew that for the dairyman each cow was different and unique, but for my untrained eye they all looked identical except for the shape of their spots.

We were showing our draft horses for a few years with some success in hitch classes when, for the first time, I saw a mare at halter which I could see "was different". I felt this mare had a presence and quality that I could recognize. It was at the Detroit International and I ran to get Mary so she could see that mare before she left the ring. The mare was College Lynda, a foundation mare of Reggie Black's very successful breeding program, and she was the Champion mare at Detroit that year. The point of the story is that if you keep studying and looking and asking questions you will begin to be able to pick out at least the top and bottom of a large class even though you might still get lost in the middle.

In summary we find that **Ideal Breed Type** does not exist as an objective standard except in the mind of the judge. You are free to establish your own ideal, and if it happens to correspond with that of the judge, in the absence of any defects, you should win. Good luck.

BREED DIFFERENCES WHEN SHOWING

The procedures for showing Belgians and Percherons are the same. The horses are groomed, fit, decorated, and shown the same.

There are some differences when showing Clydesdales and Shires. These differences are indicated, where appropriate, throughout this book.

It also would be helpful for those who plan to show Clydes and Shires to get and follow the instructions in Marion Young's two booklets, *A Beginner's Guide to Basic Conformation and Judging of Clydesdales*, and *A Beginner's Guide to Basic Show Preparation and Showmanship of Clydesdales*. Those living in the United States can get these booklets from the Clydesdale Breeders of the United States. Canadians might find it handier to get them directly from Marion Young. See Appendix II for details on how to get these two booklets.

The American Shire Horse Association has published a list of rules and guidelines for showing Shires in their quarterly Newsletter. I have reproduced most of that list in Appendix VI at the end of this book.

Dave Adams showed one of the best Percheron hitches in the 1980s, a period when the best Percheron hitches were usually the best hitches, period. The picture of his six was taken at the Belvidere, Illinois show in 1982. Ed Carlson is riding with Dave.

Paul Cooper imported more than 100 Clydesdales from Scotland, and was the premier Clyde showman at halter in the 1980s. His horses were consistent winners, and most other Clyde exhibitors were happy to get F.A.C., First After Cooper. Paul also set new standards for grooming and presentation of his horses in the showring. Here he is showing at the National Clydesdale Show in Milwaukee in 1979.

Chapter Three
Expectations

CONSISTENCY IS IMPORTANT

It's not easy to judge a draft horse show. At the smaller shows you often have the different breeds shown together, which makes judging difficult. In the larger shows you often have huge class sizes which can wear down a judge when they all have to be placed.

It is more important for a judge to be decisive and consistent than **correct. Correct,** after all, is a subjective designation and not an absolute quality. Showing under a judge that seems unable to make up his/her mind is torture. A good judge will be sure of what he likes, and will be consistent in picking it out as he judges the class. You might not agree with him but if he is decisive and consistent you have nothing to complain about.

You should put the ribbons you won in the individual classes on the halter of your horses when you bring them back out for the group classes. At the end of the show the judge is getting tired and it only makes sense to give him all the help you can. You may not be happy with the ribbon you got earlier but it is mean-spirited not to show it and hope the judge makes an error in your favor in the groups. Of course if your class ribbons are purple, blue, or red it is to your advantage to show them in the group classes.

> Judging is not easy. What is most important is that the judge be decisive and consistent.

HALTER VS. HITCHING

Most people need to make a decision which type of showing they will concentrate on, halter or hitching. It is a weakness in our system of judging that many of the horses that do well in the halter classes do not show well in harness. It is, of course, easier and cheaper to show at halter than in harness. Since you don't need show harness or vehicles when showing at halter, it is the way most people start. But I think halter is the hardest to do successfully, at least in the top shows.

Randy Robinson and Craig Grange do a little visiting after their geldings were placed at the top of a very large class at the Belgian Championship II show in 1992.

Horse breeding is not an activity that leads to instant gratification.

The very best animals are the result of breeding one outstanding individual to another outstanding individual — combined with a period of time and lots of good luck. These animals are planned, not found. They are generally raised by a family with a long tradition of raising good horses. These families treasure their best animals — especially their mares — and they are seldom for sale. And in the rare cases where these good mares are sold, the buyer is generally not a newcomer to draft horses. It is easier to buy an outstanding stallion, or stallion prospect, than an outstanding mare. You can take that outstanding stallion and breed it to your best mares and gradually improve your herd, but it is a long, slow process. Horse breeding is not an activity that leads to instant gratification. This makes it difficult to buy top halter horses, and it takes a lot of time and money to raise them.

I also think that halter judging is usually more subjective than hitch judging. Conversely, hitch judging is more objective than

Darrell Madson, assisted by Dean Woodbury, drives the Sterling six of Percheron geldings from the ring at the Live Oak show in 1993.

halter judging, especially in the smaller hitch classes (cart and team) where the action and movement of the individual horses can be seen easily. There are more close decisions in halter classes than in hitch classes. When the decision is very close the judge will tend to favor the more well-known or established breeder over the newcomer.

But I don't want to sound too pessimistic. You can exert some control over your showing success when you decide which shows to attend. The top halter horses in the land will probably not be at your local county fair. And that's where most people get started. Many horses that are placed in the bottom half of their class at the Detroit International have previously been winners at their local and even regional shows.

The type of showing you do will, in the end, be dictated by the type of horse you have available to show. We found that mares with larger feet, fewer sidebones, and cleaner hocks tended to be placed above ours in the halter classes. But there were few mares who had the action, presence, and heads-up appearance of our mares in harness. Therefore we gradually drifted away from halter showing except at the smaller shows, and instead concentrated on showing in the hitch classes. In the end you have to do the best you can with what you have.

David Helmuth and Vikki Thompson leave the ring with the Country Hitch six at the 1992 Belgian Championship II show. The next year David and Vikki took the Country Hitch, renamed the Reminisce Hitch, on a walk all the way across the United States—and got married along the way.

The dominant six horse hitch in the early 1990s was shown by Windmill Acres, owned by Edd Sigmon and driven by Joe Detweiler. Riding with Joe at Britt in 1991 is Kim Sigmon and at Davenport in 1992 is John Sigmon.

Chapter Four
Planning Ahead

LEADING UP TO THE SHOW

The first and most obvious thing to do is to decide where and when you will be showing your horses. There are so many shows to pick from these days that you can be selective about where to show. Don't bother with those shows where the management does not seem to care if you come or not. Go where you are appreciated, by both the show management and the spectators.

Although there are a lot of shows it's sometimes hard to learn about them — where and when they are. Many of the larger shows are advertised in the *Draft Horse Journal.* I have listed some of the bigger shows (those involved in the All-American contest), in Appendix IV. But there are literally hundreds of draft horse shows that are not advertised and are not well known. The best way to find out about these local, less well-known shows is just to ask someone who shows draft horses.

> There are many shows to pick from. So go where you are appreciated.

The biggest and best show is the Michigan Great Lakes International. It was held in Detroit for the first 20 years, and now, since 1997, has moved to Lansing (Michigan). Held in mid-October, it is the "World Series" of draft horse shows. The Ohio and Indiana State Fairs also have very large draft horse shows. And the Percheron and Belgian folks put on a breed show every two or three years that is huge — The Percheron Congress and the Belgian Championship Show.

You are not just restricted to showing your horses at draft horse shows. There are many Combined Driving Events and Pleasure Driving Shows which welcome draft horses even though they are primarily a light horse activity. These shows usually involve some

Here Lester Collins is exhibiting at the My Lady's Manor Pleasure Driving Show in York County (Penn.), a pleasure driving show sanctioned by the American Driving Society.

ring classes, but they also include individual workouts in a marathon course, hazards which must be navigated, and fun classes with cones. When you show draft horses at one of these driving shows you will often be a big hit with the spectators — because your horses are different. A good way to find out about driving shows is to join the American Driving Society (see Appendix I).

It is so easy to miss getting your entries in on time. Everyone does it sometime.

Let's say that your first show will be your local county fair in August. Chances are you have attended that particular show in the past, as a spectator. Months before the show you must start a regular worming, shoeing, conditioning, and training program.

All your horses should be wormed throughout the year, on a regular basis, using Ivermectin or some other worming program recommended by your veterinarian. Each spring (April?) all the horses should have a four-way shot (sleeping sickness, tetanus, influenza, and rhino). Depending on your location you may want to add a shot for Potomac Horse Fever — ask your vet. You may also want to have coggins test blood samples drawn at the same time for the horses which will be leaving the farm, depending on the specific regulations for your show. Coggins tests commonly have to be taken within six months of the show, so you may want to delay that a few months if your show season extends into the late fall. Check the health regulations for your show.

Make notes now on your calendar of the actual show dates and another note at least a week before the show entries should be mailed. It is very easy to miss the due date for making show entries — many potential exhibitors make this mistake each year. On the other hand, making entries months before the show is not practical either because horses get sick or die and your plans may change.

Some entry blanks ask you to specify the horse you are entering in each halter class. In those cases you must be the legal owner of the horse you are going to show when you fill out the entry form. Other entry blanks just ask you

The Koopman Dairy entry made a fine showing at the 1992 Santa Ynez (Calif.) Valley Carriage Classic show, another example of draft horses participating in shows that are primarily light-horse pleasure driving shows.

to indicate the classes you will enter. In those cases you must be the owner of the horse you are going to show when arriving at the showgrounds. If you are going to borrow a horse from another exhibitor (for a group class or a hitch class) you should make sure it is allowed in the show rules or ask permission to do so when you make your entries.

Your show horses may need more grain to get them in "show condition" (halter horses are generally shown a little fatter than might be normal at home). It is impossible for me to suggest a proper feeding program as it will be dictated by what feeds you have available, the age and condition of the horse, and the work or exercise it will be getting. Each horse is different. This is something you will have to work out yourself based on good management practices.

In April or May you will want to put shoes on your show horses so that they will have time to grow out a nice big foot before the show. Usually a thinner (5/16") plate is used at this time, just to protect the hoof and keep it from beaking up.

As summer rolls around you may want to keep your horses inside during the day and turn them out at night to keep their haircoat from becoming faded, burned, and dried-out in the sun. If mosquitoes are a problem you might wait until 10:00 p.m. to turn them out as the mosquitoes are less active in the late evening. A separate pen for each show horse is the ideal

Keep your show horses out of the sun as much as possible. Sun will fade and dry out their skin and coat.

Steve Gregg is driving the Harry Farr four of Belgian geldings at the 1992 National Belgian Show.

arrangement to prevent injuries when two or more horses are together. A separate pen will also save a few shoes from coming off. It's absolutely amazing how a tossed shoe can disappear in a pasture.

Yellow stains on white feather must be prevented. They will not wash out.

If you are showing Clydes or Shires with white "feather" on their legs you will have to take special precautions to protect these long hairs and to keep them clean. Yellow stains on the feather will not wash out — they must be prevented from happening in the first place. Several months before showtime you should apply a mixture of mineral oil and sulphur powder to the feather, working it into the hairs and down to the skin. This will keep the feather silky and tend to prevent staining. If your horse is kept in a box stall you will want to pick up the manure at least twice a day — some Clyde exhibitors pick up manure five and six times a day! Horses out on pasture are less likely to pick up stains, but are more likely to lose shoes, become sunburned, etc.

Horses that are going to be shown in harness must be broke, trained and conditioned. Even if your horses are well broke they still must be trained to work together and conditioned. An unconditioned horse will tire quickly, even when just pulling a cart or wagon in the showring.

Kim Sigmon drives the Windmill Acres gelding unicorn at the 1993 Wisconsin State Fair. Riding with Kim is her husband, John Sigmon.

About two months before the show your horses should be groomed and worked on a regular basis (several times a week). If they are to be shown at halter they should be set up, moved, and set up again, over and over, until the routine becomes second nature. Foals and yearlings will need frequent, but short, sessions. Horses (like people) are creatures of habit, and you need to teach them the habits they will need in the showring.

If your horses are to be shown in harness they should be driven on a regular basis, including trips on the road or in other strange situations wherever possible. Make sure your practice harness is of the same design, and with the same parts, as you will be using with your show harness. One year at the Detroit show we had a young horse who kept bucking and hopping all the way around the ring as she was driven in the unicorn class. It was only later that we realized that this was the first time she had worn a crupper, and it was bothering her. When we got home we added cruppers to all of our work harness.

If you have access to a qualified draft horse farrier you should consider yourself fortunate. Treat him well.

Horses that are normally kept in box stalls must be taught to use tie stalls and cross ties. It is better to do this at home rather than at the show.

About a month before the show you should start brushing your show horses daily, including their manes and tails. This is also the time to teach them how to take a bath if this is not part of their normal routine at home. A little mane and tail braiding at home is also a good idea.

You might also want to take your show horses to another event prior to the show. A small-town July 4th parade or an open horse show can be used to get your show

Alan Frietag drives the Live Oak Plantation entry to a first place in the Unicorn class at the 1991 National Clydesdale Show. Riding with Alan is Chester Weber.

horses accustomed to different situations. Many exhibitors go to one or more small county fairs in late June and early July to get their horses "tuned up" before starting the state fair circuit in late summer.

The plates you put on in late Spring to protect your horse's feet need to be replaced with show shoes a week or two before the show. This should be done, if at all possible, by a professional farrier who is knowledgeable about shoeing draft horses for a show. As an owner you should be willing and able to replace a shoe that comes off, or even to put the plates on your horses, but you should not tackle the job of shoeing for the show. If you have access to an experienced farrier who can do this job you should count yourself fortunate, and should treat him right. This includes calling to make an appointment well in advance, being on hand to help the whole time he is at your farm, and paying him before he leaves. Two of our sons are farriers, and it is not an easy occupation. Just to avoid some unnecessary phone calls I should also add that my sons shoe mostly Saddlebreds, and they do not do draft horses.

It is a good practice to give your horses another equine influenza (flu) shot a couple of weeks before the show. This is especially desirable if they will be gone from home for a week or more, either at a long show or at several shows, one after another. It can't hurt, and it might help keep them from coming home with an infection. Young horses are especially susceptible to catching a respiratory infection at the show.

Some exhibitors switch their show horses from their normal grain mixture to a beet pulp/oat/bran mixture about a week before the first show, and then continue to use it at the show. This is basically a filling type of feed which will keep your horses feeling full without the calories they don't need while standing in a stall.

Don Schneckloth and his unicorn at the 1982 Britt (Iowa) show.

Some exhibitors believe that this mixture, along with a switch from legume to grass hay, will reduce the tendency for a horse to fill his hocks while at the show. If you want to follow this procedure you should switch over gradually (as with any change of feed to horses) at home rather than abruptly at the show.

Several days before the show you should clip your horses heads and ears (unless you are showing Clydes or Shires). This subject, as well as others touched on in this Chapter, is treated in more detail later in this book.

Just before leaving for the show (the same day or the day before) your horses should have another bath. You want them looking as nice as possible as they leave the trailer and are put in their stalls. Remember this is a **SHOW,** and the **SHOWING** starts the minute you drive onto the showgrounds.

Unless you have a checklist, and follow it, you will leave some vital item at home.

SHOW CHECKLIST

Taking horses away from home to a show, even just to a one-day show, is a daunting event. It is essential that you develop, and follow, a checklist to make sure you bring everything that you will need. Even if the show is just a few miles from home, and someone will be going home each night, a checklist is necessary. Without a checklist you will forget something. Even with a checklist you will probably forget something but the chances are lower.

Each exhibitor will have to make his own list. To help you make yours I have reproduced in Appendix III the checklist which we used when we were showing. It should be easier for you to add or subtract from this list than to make a new one, at least for the first show.

The most important thing to wear when showing a draft horse in harness is a smile, and Mindy Griffen always did just that. Here she is driving at the 1992 National Clydesdale Show where she won the Mare Cart class.

Harold Schumacher drives his six of Percherons at the 1993 Ocala (Florida) show.

Fran and Karyn Gross are exhibiting their four abreast in front of the grandstand at the Walworth County (Wisconsin) Fair.

Chapter Five
Equipment

GENERAL

Taking a horse away from home, particularly if you will be gone overnight for one or more days, requires that you take along a lot of *stuff.* You will need feed, bedding, and tools and utensils for feeding, watering, and cleaning. A two-wheeled wheelbarrow or cart is a big help with the stall cleaning chores. Hay bags are useful if your horse is to be kept overnight in a slip stall. You will need hoses, spray nozzles, brushes, scrapers, shampoo, combs, and whatever else you use for grooming. It would be a good idea to pack an equine thermometer and some penicillin and syringes.

If you plan to do a lot of showing it may be handy to get duplicates of a lot of these tools and store these duplicates in the horse trailer. This simplifies the job of packing and unpacking significantly.

You will need a set (or several) of clothes for showing. It is not appropriate to show in your blue jeans and/or regular barn clothes. More on this later in the section on showing.

You will need a way to get to the show. This is a big subject. Rather than cover your options here please refer to the next chapter which deals with Transportation.

HALTER SHOWING

For showing at halter you will need a show halter. If you have one for each horse you are showing it will save time, eliminating the need to adjust the halters between classes. Percherons and Belgians are shown in white leather show halters. Clydesdales and Shires are shown in a white rope halter (mares) and a brown or black leather show halter (stallions and geldings).

Stallions, and mares that need a little more restraint, are often

Orndorff's Supreme U-2, Sr. Champion Stallion at the 1992 Belgian Championship II show, wearing a white leather bridle, bit in his mouth, and a lead chain under his chin.

shown in a show bridle with a straight bit and a chain under the horse's chin.

You will need a whip with a short to medium tail for following behind your horse. (If you are showing in Canada, or under a Canadian judge, you should not use a whip person or a whip.)

You will need a show stick. These vary a great deal, from fancy ones turned on a lathe to plain ones that are made from a piece of broom handle. I've seen some that are made from a piece of solid white electric fence post with a black rubber handle, or you can cut off an 18" length of a whip handle. Some harness shops carry show sticks you can buy.

If you are showing a stallion you will need two strips of contrasting colored fabric and some flowers for rolling the mane. A double knit fabric works well for the mane roll. Mares are not normally shown with a roll in their mane, but with Clydesdales and Shires this is optional. There are several people who sell draft horse decorations if you do not want to make them (See Appendix II). This is discussed more in Chapter Ten.

A spotted harness is great for parades, sleigh rallys, and field days, but is not appropriate for shows. For a field day the scotch housings should be left off the collars and the horses should not be braided.

HITCHING

HARNESS. You will need a show harness if you are going to hitch. A show harness is trimmed with shiny patent leather and chromed hardware and decorations. It is put on the horse in individual parts (collar, backpad, belly band, breeching, hames, tugs, and bridle).

A spotted harness (one decorated with many round chromed spots) is fine for parade and hay rides, but it should not be used in the showring. (Alright, if a spotted harness is all you have, and you are showing in a local or small show, go ahead and use it. But you should have a proper show harness for a larger show such as a State Fair or shows such as the Great Lakes International, Royal Winter Fair, or Denver shows.)

Show hames are elongated and chromed. You should use a scotch collar with a pointed peak and a swinging decoration at the top. You can save a little money on the collars by using a scotch housing that is strapped around an ordinary collar, making the collar appear to be a scotch collar. If you decide to do this **make sure your collar is made with an extra deep and wide hame bed behind the collar rim to accommodate both the scotch housing and the hames**. This type of collar is commonly called a *Show Collar*. We used regular farm collars with the scotch housings at our first show and when the team backed the hames came loose from the collar and ended up halfway up the horses' necks. Not good.

Harness with brass trim (instead of chrome) is more expensive and harder to clean (the brass must be polished), but it is lovely on a brown horse such as a Belgian or Clyde.

The wagon owned by Tom Justin is typical of the fine, professionally made wagons in use today. It is painted a bright yellow.

Justin Mischka showing Mi Karla at the Belvidere show.

Harness made from synthetic materials are usually lighter, stronger, and easier to care for than harness made from leather. These alternate materials vary from brightly colored nylon to the Zilco® harness that looks like leather and is being used in international driving competitions. Fine harness for the showring is traditionally made from leather but some of the better synthetic harness could be used for parades or field days. I personally dislike the brightly colored nylon harness.

If you are showing a mare in cart you can use a breast strap style of harness, rather than a collar. A breast strap harness would not be appropriate for a gelding or a stallion — or for any hitch that has two or more horses.

You should always carry a whip when driving horses.

You will need a driving whip. You should never drive a horse without a whip in your hand or somewhere handy, like in a nearby whip holder. When driving a larger hitch the whip is often on the seat behind the teamster since he already has his hands full with the many lines.

VEHICLES. If you are going to show in hitch classes you will need a vehicle — something for your horse(s) to pull and for you to sit upon.

You will probably start by showing in cart. In this case you may be able to borrow a show cart from someone at the show. This needs to be arranged beforehand, not at the show. If the breeds are being shown separately and your friend is showing a different breed from yours, or if your friend is showing a different sex (either horse or driver), it may be possible to borrow his cart.

If you are buying a show cart, get one that is easy to get into. A split seat where one-half of the seat is hinged and can be moved out of the way, and where you can enter easily from the back when the seat is moved to the out-of-way position, is good. A cart where you have to climb over the wheel and jump into the seat is dangerous, especially for a lady wearing a skirt or dress. Used show carts can be purchased at many draft horse auctions. There are many people who manufacture new show carts. There is a booklet called *The Reach* which lists many manufacturers of carts. This booklet can be purchased from the Mischka Farm bookstore (see Appendix I).

The seat on the cart should be set up high. A low seat which restricts your view to the horse's butt, and where you have to look up to even see that, is both unattractive and dangerous.

You should have another cart you can use for practicing at home. We had an ugly all-metal cart with pneumatic tires for teaching our horses to drive at home. But even when you use a practice cart at home you still should hitch to the show cart a few times before going to the show. There will be enough new things for your horse to get accustomed to without adding a new cart to the experience.

Another view of the Tom Justin wagon shown first on page 37, this time from the back.

Wagons that are painted a light color seem to show up better in the ring, especially the indoor rings.

If you are going to hitch a team (or more) you will need a show wagon. Most people use a wagon built along the lines of the old horse-drawn delivery wagons, now commonly known as hitch wagons. But any fifth-wheel wagon will do. A fifth-wheel wagon has a pin above the front axle on which the entire front axle rotates. The front wheels are smaller and roll completely under the wagon box when making a sharp turn. With such a wagon you can swing the team completely around so that they face the rear of the wagon.

If you page through a book like *Heroes in Harness* you will see examples of the many types of fifth-wheel wagons that have been used in the past, ranging from milk wagons and other light delivery wagons to large, heavy-duty moving vans.

The size and type of vehicle should fit the size of hitch (number of horses) you plan to drive. Four or six horses would be as inappropriate on a light delivery wagon as a pair would be on a large hitch wagon.

Most hitch wagons have wooden wheels, and the newer ones are outfitted with hydraulic brakes and roller bearings. Some exhibitors use a smaller wagon with rubber tires that can towed behind a vehicle, eliminating the need to transport it in a truck or on a trailer. These rubber-tired wagons work fine for a team but the teamster is usually sitting down too low for good visibility when driving more than a pair.

I have always felt that light-colored wagons look better (show up better in the ring) than do dark-colored ones. Our wagon was a bright yellow, and if I were to do it again I would stay with that color. White is another good hitch wagon color. Dark colors such as black, dark red, and dark blue do not show up well in an inside arena.

You can get a used (or new) hitch wagon at many draft horse auctions or you can have a new wagon built by one of the many people in that business (See Appendix V). If you are on a limited budget and/or are an experienced woodworker you can buy a used running gear and some new wheels and build your hitch wagon, which is what we did.

If you decide to build your own box you might cover the outside of the sides with a material like masonite before painting. We found it's very difficult to get a smooth surface on plywood or other lumber.

Sheila Junkans drives a team of Percherons, part of the Ames hitch, out of the ring at the 1993 Wisconsin State Fair.

Chapter Six
Transportation

GENERAL

Hauling horses in a truck or trailer is an unnatural act. I don't know anyone who actually enjoys it. We have all heard horror stories of accidents while hauling horses. But hauling horses is a necessary evil when showing horses.

It is difficult to raise horses, or even to just own them, without also having the means to move them about. But it can be done. Some folks get by with a helpful neighbor who has a truck and trailer and is willing to haul their horses. Others will use a professional horse hauler. But most of us end up, sooner or later, buying a vehicle to haul our horses.

It is difficult to raise horses, or just to own them, without having the means to move them about.

EQUIPMENT

Most folks start with a two-horse trailer pulled behind a car or truck they already own. This works out fine for riding horses, but is less desirable, and a little dangerous, for draft horses. It is better to use a gooseneck fifth wheel trailer behind a pick up truck (rather than a bumper hitch) with draft horses because of the added weight involved.

If you are going to show more than two horses, or going to show in both halter and harness, additional hauling capacity is needed. If your first harness classes are going to be in cart you might be able to postpone buying and hauling the cart by borrowing one at the show. This is often done. Even then it would be best to have your own harness.

We started with a two-horse bumper trailer. Next we went to a four-horse gooseneck behind a crew-cab pickup. This was followed by a large dropped-bed semi-trailer pulled behind a single axle tractor. We finished by using a seven-horse slant load gooseneck behind a diesel pickup. Like most things in life, we all seem to have to make our own mistakes and learn things for ourselves.

The semi-tractor we bought must have been intended to move trailers around in a trucker's yard, as it had only a 20 gallon gas tank. When you get only 6 miles to a gallon that 20 gallons gets used very quickly. We needed a bumper sticker that said "I brake for gas stations." I added a second tank to solve this problem but not before we had some experiences too scary and dumb to repeat here.

The semi-trailer/tractor option is quite popular with the big hitch exhibitors. You will see them lined up in the parking lot at all the major shows. Very impressive. We had our semi-trailer arranged to haul six horses, a cart and hitch wagon, feed and harness. It worked out fine, and was much cheaper to buy (used) and to outfit than a large horse trailer and good pickup. But I was never comfortable driving it. There are lots of added regulations to follow, a commercial driver's license is needed, a log book must be kept, and you don't dare skip any weigh stations. For several years after we sold our semi tractor and trailer I continued to be pestered by several states for fuel taxes they thought I might owe them. I believe that the semi-trailer approach to hauling horses is a good one when you have a need for that equipment elsewhere in your business. Otherwise it seems to me that the extra hassles with a semi made the horse hauling experience even more worrisome than it was normally.

> Most horse trailers are not wide or high enough to haul draft horses in comfort or safety.

If you go the semi-trailer approach the trailer should have a drop-bed where there is a step down from the fifth wheel area to the balance of the trailer, making the ramp up into the trailer less steep. An air-ride trailer with air-bags between the axle and the floor of the trailer will give a smoother ride.

The outfit we ended up with was a seven horse slant-load aluminum gooseneck behind a 3/4 ton truck. This worked out fine for us though I would go with gas instead of diesel next time as the fuel savings are not worth the loss in acceleration. One person can load and unload horses easily with the modern slant-load trailers. Make sure you get thick rubber matting on the floor and sides of the trailer. Or you can have a thick coating of Rhino Lining® sprayed on the floor and sides of your trailer, instead of the rubber mats. I have this sprayed material in the bed of my

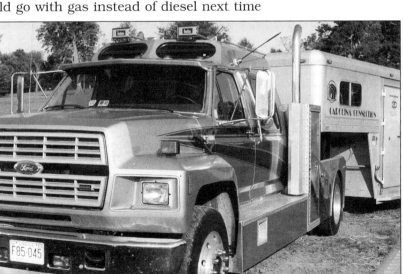

The folks and horses from Carolina Connection travel in style to the horse pulls at which they participate.

current pickup truck and like it very much. The stalls should be at least 36" wide, and the height of the trailer should be at least 7-1/2 feet. The trailer width should be as wide as the trailer company can legally make it. **Most conventional horse trailers, built for riding horses, are not wide or high enough for draft horses to ride in comfortably.** I prefer a trailer with a ramp. With a ramp the horses will walk into the trailer easier and there is less chance for injury (feet sliding under the trailer floor when unloading). But the ramp has to be strong and stiff. If the ramp flexes when the horses step on it they will tend to balk and not want to load.

Your pickup truck has to have a rated towing capacity that is sufficient for the load you plan to pull. **This means you have to decide on the type of trailer you will use (bumper hitch or 5th wheel gooseneck) and calculate the probable weight of the loaded trailer before you buy the truck.**

We used a second pickup pulling a flat-bed trailer for the wagon, harness boxes, and cart. It gets involved, and expensive.

REGULATIONS

We live in a very regulated society. It is virtually impossible to be completely legal at all times. This is especially true when driving a vehicle hauling horses. A policeman who had a fight with his wife before leaving for work or an inspector who is anxious to display his power and knowledge can always find something wrong which needs a ticket. As with an income tax audit you just hope they find something quickly, and that it isn't too serious, so they will go on to bother someone else.

FEDERAL SAFETY REGULATIONS FOR COMMERCIAL VEHICLES

Generally speaking, if the combined gross (loaded) weight of your truck and trailer is less than 10,000 pounds you are not subject to the federal rules regarding Commercial vehicles and you do not need a Commercial Driver's License. This would include many people hauling two riding horses, but most rigs hauling two adult draft horses would go over 10,000 pounds.

If your combined gross weight is between 10,001 and 26,000 pounds, and you stay within your state, you are again exempt from these federal rules. If you are in this weight category and travel interstate (from one state to another) you must decide if you are a "Commercial Vehicle". This is a subjective determination. Some officers will consider any trailer with the farm name painted on the side to be a Commercial Vehicle. Others will assume that anyone who is spending so much money on trailers and trucks

There are so many regulations and rules that it is virtually impossible to be completely legal at all times.

must be making money with their horses, making it a commercial activity. If you decide you are recreational (not commercial) and an enforcement official disagrees, and gives you a ticket, you can later argue your case in court. The point of this "Commercial Vehicle" designation is that drivers of Commercial Vehicles must have a Commercial Driver's License and are bound by the Federal Motor Carrier Safety Regulations which require special vehicle markings, a medical card, a log book, and an inspection sticker.

If your combined gross weight (truck, trailer, and contents) exceeds 26,001 pounds you are, by definition, a Commercial Vehicle subject to the Federal Motor Carrier Safety Regulations written for such vehicles.

State regulations are at least as restrictive as federal regulations but, in some cases, they are even more restrictive.

WEIGH STATIONS

Practically speaking, unless you are breaking a traffic law while driving, the only places that you are likely to be stopped for an examination of your license and other papers is at a weigh station. There is a lot of confusion as to who must stop and who can drive on by. The rules vary from state to state. The examples in the following paragraph will illustrate the complexity of this situation.

In Ohio any vehicle pulling a trailer with a gross vehicle weight of 6,000 pounds or more must stop. In Pennsylvania all trucks, regardless of size, must stop. In New Hampshire all horse trailers must stop. In Michigan any vehicle with dual tires must stop. Florida weigh stations are also Agricultural Stations, and any vehicle with a horse inside must stop. In Kansas and Indiana all trucks, including pick-ups, are required to stop.

In actual practice most people assume that the word "TRUCK" when used at a weigh station means semi-tractors. If they are driving a pick-up they usually drive on by without pulling in. It's also true that when a pick-up pulls into a weigh station they are often waved through. But on the other hand, we all have heard of cases where a squad car has sped out of a weigh station, caught a pick-up truck which had driven by without stopping, and brought him back for a full inspection and citations. It's up to you, as the driver, whether or not you want to take the chance.

HEALTH AND OTHER PAPERS

Virtually every state requires a current (6 or 12 months) negative EIA (Coggins) test to accompany any horse moved into

> Unless you are speeding the only time you are likely to be stopped for an examination is at a weigh station.

This is a drop-bed trailer — the floor of the trailer is lower than the area which rests on the fifth wheel. The horses are side loaded, and the wagon is loaded in the back using an electric winch to pull it up the ramp.

another state. A current (commonly 10 days) CVI (Certificate of Veterinary Inspection or Health Paper) usually must accompany horses traveling from one state to another. You also should keep a copy of your proof of insurance card and vehicle registration certificates with you when traveling, especially out-of-state. A copy of the Registration Certificates for the horses you are hauling, or some other proof of ownership, is also a good idea to have along.

SAFETY CONSIDERATIONS

You are required to meet the safety requirement of the states in which you travel. Ohio was one of the first states to require an independent break-away braking system on horse trailers. That year, many exhibitors were stopped as they entered Ohio on the way to the state fair and were forced to have these systems installed on their trailers before they could continue. Other trailer safety equipment which may be required are safety chains, brakes on all wheels, and specific running lights and reflectors. The trailer you buy may be legal for these safety items where and when it was built, but may be deficient where or when you plan to travel.

It goes without saying that your trailer floor, especially if it is wood, should be inspected for weak spots. We all know of horror stories where the trailer floor gave out during a trip and the horse that dropped through the floor was killed or severely injured. (I also remember one where the horse straddled the hole and arrived at the destination unharmed.)

Tires are another part of the trailer that should be inspected. Good tires are a good investment. A flat tire on a busy highway with a trailer full of horses is no fun. It is also dangerous.

Trailer wheels should be removed and the bearings packed with grease at least once a year, depending on the amount of use your trailer gets.

And the inside of the trailer should be checked for loose or sharp objects that could injure your horse.

MANAGEMENT CONSIDERATIONS

Horses seem to know, instinctively, that hauling them in a vehicle is unnatural. You should give them a short, trial run in the trailer prior to showtime. It may take a while to get them loaded the first time or two, and it's best to be teaching them to load on a day when you have some extra time rather than on showday.

A good experience for the horseman is to take a short ride in the horsetrailer, without a horse. It is surprising how noisy and frightening a ride it can be. After such an experience you will likely be a smoother and less aggressive driver, making smoother turns and stops.

Take a short ride in your horse trailer without your horse — it will make you a better driver.

There are many techniques that can be used to get horses used to loading. Putting a horse that is used to being hauled in first will help ease the fears of a new one. Parking the trailer in the lot or pasture where the horses stay may help them get accustomed to it, but may also be hard on the trailer. Grain can be used to coax some horses inside a trailer. The threat or noise from a whip sometimes helps. The main thing is to take it easy. Getting angry will usually make the job much harder.

Horses do not like to enter a dark space. They often load easier in a stock trailer because stock trailers have open spaces in their sides and are not as dark inside as a conventional trailer. You can let more light into your conventional trailer by opening the escape door at the front of the trailer, but make sure that the loaded horse cannot get to that open doorway. Our Arab mare once jumped into the trailer at the back and then proceeded to jump

Another drop-bed trailer hooked to a dual axle tractor. Harness is carried in the boxes under the trailer.

out the escape door at the front. If your trailer has interior lights you should turn them on. This may require having the trailer hooked to your truck, with the electrical cable connected. Having the trailer hooked before loading the horses is a good idea in any event. It makes it possible to start out quicker and it makes the trailer more stable during loading.

I am reading a lot lately about the alleged advantages of hauling horses backwards. Advocates of this method claim that horses can be left untied, and then are able to keep their balance by raising or lowering their heads rather than leaning into the trailer. Studies have shown that horses hauled backwards arrive with lower pulse and heart rates, and are more relaxed. But if you decide to haul them backwards you should make sure that your trailer is built with this in mind. The trailer axle must be moved back on a two-horse bumper-hitch trailer to compensate for the fact that a horse carries 65% of his weight on his front legs.

After the horses are loaded you should start out on the trip as soon as possible. Standing still with loaded horses at the start of a trip just makes them nervous and they start to paw and bang up the trailer. Stop after driving 15 minutes or so and get out to take a look to make sure they are doing alright. Check again in an hour if the trip will be several hours long. If the weather is hot you should open all windows and vents to make sure they are getting plenty of air. Even in the winter you want to make sure they get enough air so that it doesn't become a sauna inside the trailer, especially when they are nervous and steaming.

Load a single horse travelling in a two horse trailer on the left side, or if you are hauling two horses in a two horse trailer then load the heavier horse on the left side. This is because most roads have a crown in the middle and if your load is heavy on the right side the trailer is less stable. This is also true if you have to go on the shoulder, either deliberately or accidentally.

You can often use a single axle tractor to pull your horse trailer. This is the tractor used by the Hale Brothers.

Plan to stop every two hours or so and take a short break. This gives the horse(s) a chance to relax and urinate. Horses will seldom urinate while you are moving. And if you walk around every two hours or so you will be less likely to develop a potentially serious blood clot in your leg.

If the trip will be for more than an hour you should put some bedding such as shavings (without dust) over the rubber mats. Many horses will refuse to urinate on a bare floor.

If the trip will take more than 12 hours you should find somewhere to stop, unload, and let the horses rest during the trip rather than driving straight through.

Hot weather hauling is very tough on horses. Make sure they are getting all the air that is possible considering the construction of your trailer. When you stop for gas or meals you should open doors and other openings in the trailer. Offer the horses a drink of water, though they probably will refuse it. Travel at night when it is cooler if at all possible.

If you are travelling with more than one vehicle in a caravan, a couple of CB radios are very useful in maintaining contact between the drivers.

These are the harness boxes standing along the side of the Wayne & Earlene Laursen trailer. The hitch wagon goes in next. The cart is typically transported by hanging it above the wagon or by putting it into the gooseneck.

I have not tried to provide the reader with a full explanation of the laws and regulations that govern the hauling of horses. My purpose has only been to show that the subject is more complicated than they might have first thought. And, as with most areas of legislation, it is constantly changing.

Much of the information in this section has been taken from a booklet called "Horse Trailering on the Road." I urge the reader to get a current copy of this booklet for information specific to his situation and location if he plans to haul horses more than 150 miles from his home. This booklet may be ordered from the Mischka Farm Bookstore (Appendix I).

Rod Derrer is one of the outstanding teamsters on the show circuit today. He, like so many others like him, started at an early age. Here he is driving a team at the 1982 Britt Show.

Gere and Sally Dearborn are leaving the ring at the 1989 Michigan Great Lakes International after winning the Percheron Mare Team class. The horses are Mi Cindy and Mi Cassandra, two mares raised and trained by the author.

Chapter Seven
Shoeing

GENERAL

Shoeing a draft horse is an art and a science — in addition to being darn hard work. Count yourself lucky if you are able to get the services of a competent, knowledgeable draft horse farrier who can provide show shoes and put them on correctly. Treat him well. Make appointments well in advance of needing him, be on hand to help when he comes to your farm, offer him lunch and keep him supplied with cold water, and **pay him before he leaves your farm**. In other words, just treat him as you would want to be treated.

Pick up, clean, and trim your horses feet on a regular basis. **It is not the job of the farrier to teach your horse to allow his feet to be picked up and worked upon — it is yours**. Anyone with draft horses should be able to trim his horses feet, tighten a loose shoe, and put a shoe back on that has been thrown. If you are unable to do this you should at least have access to someone nearby that will help you do these "maintenance" jobs. You cannot expect the farrier to come back to do these chores. He is usually too busy, and the travel time makes the trip impractical.

It is not your farrier's job to teach your horse to stand with his foot up — it is yours.

IMPORTANCE OF SHOEING FOR THE SHOW

It is generally agreed that the legs and feet are the most important parts of a draft horse. A judge might first take a quick look at the overall impression given by a horse, but he will soon concentrate on the feet and legs. He begins and ends his judging there. If he doesn't like what he sees he might not look at anything else. The importance of the feet and legs cannot be overemphasized.

The normal reasons for putting a shoe on a horse are to protect his feet from bruising or cracking. Or in the winter we might shoe a horse with a non-slip material such as borium to keep him from slipping on the ice. Shoeing a draft horse for showing, however, takes on a whole new dimension. The shoe becomes a means of enhancing the size of the hoof or

These are the front (left) and hind (right) feet of E.J.G. Barb, one of the most celebrated Belgian mares in recent years. She won without excessive flare or size to her foot. The angle of the hoof wall corresponds to the angle of the pastern, and doesn't flare out to the outside on the hind foot or to the front on the front foot.

Applying putty to a hoof to make it appear larger or to cosmetically repair a cracked or damaged hoof.

Excessive correction when shoeing will lead to joint and hoof problems in the future.

changing its shape. It also becomes a way of changing the way in which the horse stands, or its way of moving. This makes shoeing for the show so very important. Shoes properly applied can improve the appearance and way of going for most horses. The wrong shoes, or the right shoes put on incorrectly, will hurt the appearance and way of going for all horses.

CORRECTIVE SHOEING

A good deal of what we call shoeing a horse for a show is, in fact, corrective shoeing. A hoof can be made to look larger by applying a shoe that is too large for the foot, and then applying auto-body putty or other filler on the hoof wall to make it larger. Or it can be made to look larger simply by having it grow out to an excessive length by not cutting the hoof wall between shoeings. Cutting off and squaring the toe on the front can help a horse break over and move straight, reducing his tendency to wing or paddle. Cutting down the inside hoof wall and building up the outside wall on back feet will throw the hocks together. These techniques and others, used mostly on halter horses, can be abused and overdone. It's the old problem of "if a little is good then more must be better." It isn't.

Pads are used to protect the sole of the foot from bruising and, with medicated packing, to keep the foot healthy. Here again they are sometimes used as an enhancement or corrective tool, increasing apparent hoof size or increasing the length of the outside wall on the hind feet.

Excessive correction when shoeing for the show, particularly with halter horses, will invariably lead to joint and/or hoof problems in the future. You cannot nail a weight (shoe) on the end of a leg without exaggerating the movement and creating strain on the joints higher up the leg. The more you change the way in which that hoof sits on the ground when the horse is standing or the way it lands on the ground

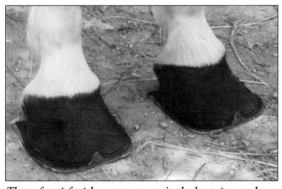

These front feet have an excessively long toe and are shod with a leather pad. The large, square-toed shoe gives an unnatural duck-bill look to the foot.

when the horse is moving (from what it would do normally without the shoe) the more likely you are to cause damage to the horse's joints and tendons.

Show horses are often shod with excessive flair and/or overly long feet. This is especially true on the outside of the back feet where this flair will move the hocks together. These techniques will inevitably lead to a separation of the hoof wall and to infection, and may result in ringbone and sidebone. The reason many top halter horses are not shown in harness is that the ridiculous shoes they are wearing will not allow them to work very long at a trot before they start interfering and bloodying their lower legs.

> Excessive flair will inevitably lead to a separation of the hoof wall.

SCOTCH BOTTOMS

People tend to call show shoes "scotch bottom shoes." The words "scotch bottom" simply mean that the edge of the shoe is sloped outwards, from top to bottom, in the same angle as the hoof wall is sloped. Most show shoes are, in fact, made with this sloping edge. It tends to finish the shoe nicely, and gives the horse a bigger surface at the bottom of his foot. But plates can also have scotch bottoms, and a show shoe could be made with a vertical outside edge.

GETTING YOUR HORSE SHOD FOR THE SHOW

Eight weeks before the show you should put light-weight shoes (plates) on your horse so that he will grow his hoof out some and to allow the elimination of any cracks or broken-out pieces from the hoof wall. You can use a keg shoe or a ⁵⁄₁₆" x 1" shoe made for that purpose. If there is quite a bit of cracking or breaking you might want to start this sooner.

After the plates are put on your horse you may want to restrict some of his movement by keeping him in a smaller pen or pasture and by keeping him separate from other horses. This will tend to keep the shoes from coming off — and if they do come off, it will make it easier to find them.

Once they are shod you should check their shoes each day, and loose shoes should be tightened as soon as they are noticed. Draft horse shoes, especially those for showing, are often larger than the foot they are nailed upon, and this makes them prone to come off. It is a lot

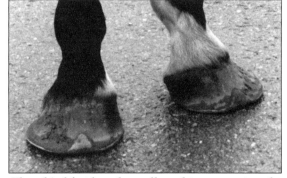

These hind feet have been allowed to grow out on the outside and the resulting flair is being repaired and accentuated with putty. This is an unbalanced foot designed to throw the hocks together. Try to resist the temptation to do this to your horse.

Drawings of front and hind show shoes. The front has a squared toe and (optional) heel caulks. The hind has a caulk on the outside branch with a thin inside branch.

easier to tighten a shoe that is getting loose than to find a thrown shoe and put it back on.

RE-SETTING SHOES

If you are going to many shows over a period of two months or more you will want to have the show shoes re-set. It "hurts" to remove and re-set shoes that are tight and good-looking, but it is much better for the horse to have them re-set than to leave them on with excessive hoof wall. You may be able to get this re-setting done at a show as many of the bigger shows will have a farrier in attendance.

SHOE REMOVAL AT THE END OF THE SHOW SEASON

When your show season is over you should remove the shoes and trim down (off) the excess hoof wall. A good time to do this is at the last show while you are waiting for the release time. At any rate, it should be done before turning the horses out to pasture when you return home. Horses that are turned out to pasture after being confined at a show and standing in a trailer ride for the ride home are usually kind of frisky. If they are still wearing their shoes they are likely to throw some shoes, which may become lost in the grass, and they may cause injuries to each other.

ADDITIONAL INFORMATION

The two main sources of draft horse shoes are The Anvil Brand Shoe Company and the Will Lent Horseshoe Company. For details see Appendix II.

Shoeing draft horses for the showring is a controversial subject. Many of the things I have advocated in this chapter are contrary to the way horses are being shod for the showring today. As further support for these suggestions I have reprinted the position of the American Shire Horse Association on correct shoeing in Appendix VII.

Will Lent is shaping a shoe while the horse's owner, Abe Allebach looks on. Will is a draft horse farrier and shoe manufacturer.

Chapter Eight
Trimming and Bathing

TRIMMING AND CLIPPING

Percherons and Belgians need to have their heads, ears, and bridle path trimmed with a small animal trimming clipper. This trimming should be done at home, just before going to the show.

The only trimming you should do on Clydes and Shires is on the ears and bridle path. Leave all the hair on the head. However, if you are showing at a small show where the breeds will be mixed, and if the judge is a Belgian or Percheron person, you might want to trim off some of the excess facial hair under the jaw of your Clyde or Shire.

The first few times you trim your horse he may object and fight you, especially when doing the ears. Just take your time, doing a little bit each time you bring the clippers up to his body, and don't get upset or angry. The clipper noise is frightening to many horses, so the quieter your clipper is the better. Make sure the clipper blades are sharp. Dull blades pull the hair, hurting the animal. Dull blades can be reconditioned and resharpened. It also helps to get the horse used to the vibration of the clipper by just putting your hand on the horse's neck, and then holding the clipper against your hand, letting the vibrations go through your hand to the horse's neck.

Your horses should be trimmed and groomed at home, before you go to the show.

You should start by removing all the long whisker hairs from around the mouth and muzzle. Then trim back the long, unruly eyebrow hairs.

If your horse has a heavy hair coat you may want to trim back some of the hair from the side of the face and from under the head and chin. You don't want to shave these areas clean, so turn the clipper over and draw it down backwards across the hairs while holding the clipper body out away from the horse. This will allow you to just cut back the longer hairs.

A nicely groomed head and mane.

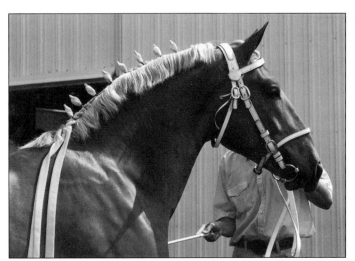

One of the Hale Brothers horses waiting to go into the showring. The Hales trim their horses' manes a little shorter than some, but their horses are impeccably well-groomed

Excess hair needs to be trimmed off the edges of the ears. If your horse objects to this it helps to stuff some cotton in his ears first. Another technique is to pinch the ears closed and then just run the clippers up the sides of the closed edges. This will leave the hairs inside the ear intact where they will continue their normal function of keeping out bugs while at the same time giving the ear a neat appearance.

Some horses simply refuse to permit the clippers to be used on their ears. For these animals you will have to use the twitch and just complete the job as quickly as possible. If they are adamant about not being clipped about their ears you will lose the battle and might get hurt in the process.

The mane should be roached where the bridle crosses it (the bridle path). A large cow clipper will work for this, or you can take small bites with the small clipper you used on the head. Cut off about four fingers of mane hair so that the bridle will sit snugly on the neck.

After a horse has had his bridle path trimmed you should take steps to make sure he does not develop a sore under the halter strap. This is especially common when your horse wears a nylon halter. It is a good idea to thread the halter strap that goes over the neck into a sheepskin or cloth tube to give some extra cushioning to compensate for the mane hair that you have removed. A halter cut on the top of the neck becomes infected easily and is difficult to cure without letting your horse go without a halter for a period of time. After such an episode your horse may well end up head-shy.

One final place you might want to clip your Percheron or Belgian is around the coronary band to show off the hoof wall and behind the leg on the cannon bone or behind the knee. Do not trim off any of the fetlock hairs.

Cathy Zahm is a professional horse trainer who is also well known for her talents in grooming draft horses. She has produced a nice video called *Grooming Tips for Show and Sale* in which she describes how she clips and grooms a draft horse for a show. We recommend this video, and it can be purchased from the Mischka

Farm Bookstore (as can each of the books and videos mentioned in this book). See Appendix I.

THINNING THE MANE AND TAIL

Some horses, especially some older horses, need to have their manes and/or tails thinned and evened. This is done by pulling hairs. **Do not cut off the mane or tail hairs with a scissors or clipper** — this leaves a straight line which looks unnatural.

To pull a mane or tail you grab the ends of just a few hairs you want to remove with your left hand. You then separate these few hairs from the rest of the hairs around them by running the fingers on your right hand up the length of the hairs you have selected to remove. Or you can back-comb the hairs you have not selected out of the way. You then twist the ends of the hairs to be removed around your fingers (or around the comb) and give a sharp yank. They will pull out. This doesn't hurt the horse, but after a time he may become bored or impatient with this procedure and you may have to quit for a while.

Pulling mane and tail hairs can be rough on your hands. Horse hair is tough, and it will cut your unprotected fingers. You should wear lightweight leather gloves at least on your right (pulling) hand.

If you have a lot to pull you should do some on each of several days. After a while the horse will get tired of having his hairs pulled. It's better to quit and finish another day than have you both get sour about it.

The finished mane, after pulling, should cover one-half to one-third of the horse's neck and should be a uniform length down the length of the neck. A mane that hides more than half the horse's neck gives a course, heavy appearance.

After pulling, the finished tail (that is not docked) should end at the hocks. It is seldom necessary to pull hairs on a docked tail.

> Manes should be shortened by pulling, not by cutting with a scissors.

This is a Clydesdale stallion from Anheuser Busch waiting his turn to go into the ring at the 1994 National Clydesdale Sale in Springfield, Illinois..

There is no dress code when it comes time to bathe your horse.

BATHING

A few people feel that bathing horses removes too many oils from their coat, and they do not bathe their horses above their knees and hocks for showing. However, most people bathe their horses. (Even those who do not bathe their horses should still wash them with an iodine medicated shampoo at least once a year to eliminate and prevent fungal and bacterial skin conditions.)

Most horses are given a good bath the day before leaving for the show. Use a mild, non-detergent shampoo and a plastic curry comb to get out all the dirt down to the horse's skin. A curry comb that screws onto the end of the hose does a good job of loosening and washing away the scale and dirt on the skin.

Stallions and geldings should have their sheath washed every month or so. Use a mild soap and small sponge to get up in there and get this area clean. Rubber or plastic gloves are a good idea to prevent your hands from picking up any strong odors and to keep your finger nails from irritating the horse.

Drying the feather with sawdust.

Horses should not be bathed on the same day they will be shown at halter. Instead bathe them the evening before which will give the hairs a chance to get re-lubricated and lay down on the skin.

Use a sweat scraper to remove some of the excess water from the horse and then spray him with Show Sheen, Laser Sheen, or some other coat polish. Use your hands to spread the polish into the coat with the grain of the hair. These polishes make the coat shine, but the oil they add also can collect dust. If you are showing a black horse in dusty conditions you may want to skip the polish. Don't spray the polish on the mane or tail if you will be braiding these as they will be too slippery to braid well.

Clydes and Shires should have dry pine sawdust rubbed into their feather after washing.

BLACKENING THE HOOVES

Belgians and Percherons are usually shown with blackened hooves, even when the hoof may be all or part white. Clydes and Shires with white hooves are generally shown with their hoof its natural color.

It is a good idea to blacken hooves while at home, after the bath when the horse has dried off. You will probably have to do it again before the class but it is good for both you and the horse to practice this at home where there are fewer distractions. It also gives the horse a nice appearance when arriving at the show.

You can use a commercially prepared hoof blackener which is sold at any tack shop or an ordinary can of black spray paint found at any hardware store. If you use the paint you should get a dull black, not a gloss black. Some people think that paint will cause the hoof to dry out and that the commercial hoof blackener is therefore better. We didn't find this to be a problem when we changed from hoof-black to the paint. The paint is cheaper and easier to use.

Jennifer Black is driving a Percheron gelding, Prince, at the 1981 Detroit International show. The cart she is using, which was built by her husband, Bob, has a seat that sits up high so she has a good view of the horse and the area in front of the horse.

Ross Beattie and his granddaughter, Emily, are on their way to winning the Belgian Mare Team class at the 1989 Michigan Great Lakes International show in Detroit.

Dave Carson and Marion Young with their winning team of Clydesdale geldings at the 1988 Boone County Fair in Belvidere, Illinois.

Chapter Nine
Arrival at the Showgrounds

SAFETY FIRST

When you arrive at the showgrounds your first concern should be for the safety and well-being of your horses. Before going off to find the location of your stalls you should check the condition of the horses in the trailer. If the weather is warm or hot, you should open some windows and/or doors in the trailer for added ventilation. Leave someone with the horses at the trailer while you go to look for the stalls.

Usually you will locate your stalls by first contacting the show or barn manager. You should bring your health papers with you in case he wants to see them before you unload your horses. He will then direct you to your stalls.

When you find your stalls you should check them all over for protruding nails or other sharp edges that might injure your horses. Run your hands over the entire inside of the stall.

Decide which stalls to use for tack and feed and which horses will go where. If you are bringing a stallion you may want him by himself, with a tack stall between him and your mares.

Check the condition of your horses just as soon as you arrive at the showgrounds.

Bed the stalls with clean straw or dustless shavings. When the floor of the (slip) stall is dirt we found it helpful to put down a thick trailer mat first, under the bedding, to keep the horses from digging a hole with their front feet. Then you are ready to unload the horses. When they are securely tied in their stalls you should leave them alone for a while until they get used to their new surroundings. Don't leave them unattended — just leave them alone.

The decorations do not have to be fancy or expensive. Here the decorations consist of a fabric strip on the stall posts and a valence above the stalls.

The canopy over the back of these stalls helps to tie everything together, and the straw out into the aisle helps keep the visitors out of kicking range of the horses. The names above the stalls are sometimes intentionally wrong so that the visitors do not confuse the horses by continually calling their names.

DECORATIONS

If you are going to be at a show for more than one day it is customary to decorate the stalls. If you have chosen particular colors for your farm it is nice to use these colors for your stall decorations. If the showgrounds are near your farm you might find it convenient to go over a day or two before you bring the horses and do the decorating then. You might also want to bed the stalls and bring your feed beforehand too.

The most commonly used decoration is a colored valence across the top of the stalls. This adds color to the barn and ties your stalls together. You should also hang cloths or sheets in front of tack and feed stalls. Bedroom stall walls should be covered on all four sides.

A picture board of your horses at home or at various horse activities can be very interesting to the other exhibitors and to the public. Since the public walking through the barn typically sees only the rear end of your horses as they stand in their stalls they will stop and examine a picture board with great interest.

Red, blue, and purple ribbons from the show you are at, or from previous shows **during the same year,** will always add a nice bit of color to your decorations.

This is one of the picture boards we hung on our stalls at the shows. People really enjoy looking at the photos.

HAY, STRAW, AND MANURE

Some of the larger shows will have hay and/or straw for sale, but very few of the smaller shows do. It is always better to bring your own, especially the hay and feed, to avoid sudden changes in diet for your horses. But if this is impractical and you want to buy it at the show you should check ahead of time to make sure it will be available. Bring at least some hay from home and switch to the purchased hay gradually.

Some horses will refuse to drink strange water at a new location — at least for a while. This can be a real problem. It is a good idea to bring a large plastic container filled with water from home for horses that refuse to drink at the show. After a day or so they will usually drink the water at the show.

Manure should be picked up from behind the horses frequently to keep the stalls nice looking and to reduce the number of flies in the barn. Rubber garbage cans placed in the aisle at the end of the stalls can be a great help when picking up manure.

> Get a two-wheeled garden cart to haul out the manure. A regular wheelbarrow tends to tip easily.

A wheelbarrow or two-wheeled cart is needed to remove manure and soiled bedding from the barn. A two-wheeled cart is much better as it holds more and is easier to wheel about. I find these carts indispensible both at the show and at home. Stalls need to be cleaned out completely every day. It is amazing how fast the bedding in a dirty stall starts to decompose and heat if it is not cleaned out every day.

HOT WEATHER PRECAUTIONS

If you are at the showgrounds during very hot weather you will want to put a large fan on each horse and make sure they are all drinking enough water. Cut back on the grain and make sure the stalls are clean and do not have manure heating up in them.

Fly spray on the aisle floor or on stall walls will help to control insects — in addition to the fly spray you normally apply to the horses.

If you have to travel in very hot weather it is best to do it at night, when it is cooler, and make sure the horses have plenty of ventilation.

EXERCISE

If you are staying overnight at the showgrounds you will have to exercise your horses to keep them

Alan Frietag taking four of Live Oak's Clydes on an early morning walk at the Detroit show. Horses that have been shown a lot tend to be well behaved on their morning stroll.

from becoming sour and crabby or from developing swelling in the hocks and ankles.

The best time to exercise your horses is in the early morning before the showgrounds become crowded. Most exhibitors have someone clean out the stalls at the same time the horses are out being exercised.

The most common way to exercise your horses is to take them for a long walk — 20 minutes or longer. If they are accustomed to being lunged, and if there is a suitable place for lunging (the showring, for example), you can give them more exercise, quicker, that way. The important thing is that they get out of their stalls for some exercise at least once a day.

FEEDING TIMES AT THE SHOW

For the most part you will not feed your horses during the day while they are in their stalls at the show. You will want to give them their grain and water in the early morning and late afternoon, and feed hay in the evening when you are going to bed. If it is hot you will want to offer them water several times during the day.

If your horses are being kept in slip stalls you will find it convenient to feed their hay in haybags. If you feed it on the ground they may kick it behind them and be unable to reach it. Make sure you tie the haybags up high so they cannot get a foot into it. Tie it securely as it will tend to come loose as the horse works to get the hay out.

Harness is heavy, unwieldy, and expensive. These harness boxes serve double duty, providing a handsome and convenient way to display the harness in a tack stall and a way to transport the harness in the truck or trailer.

If they are in box stalls you can feed hay on the ground. This is really better since they will not get so much chaff in their lungs when stretching down to eat the hay.

DEALING WITH THE PUBLIC

Many of the visitors who go through the barn are not farm folk. They will ask you why the horses are in stalls with their tails facing out (instead of with their heads facing out). They will ask about docked tails. They will ask about the breed of your horse even though it may be clearly stated on your sign. They will ask a dozen questions, over and over again. You should resist the temptation to give flippant answers to their questions. Try to give honest, sensible answers — over and over again. The person who asks you a seemingly stupid question may be a customer tomorrow. Remember, when you are at a show you are a public relations person for the draft horse community.

Except for the early morning chore-time when stalls are being cleaned, horses fed and watered, etc., the barn should be kept clean and tidy. The aisle should be clean and either raked or swept. Manure should be picked up and either removed or hidden (in containers or under bedding).

Someone should stay by the stalls, or by a group of stalls, to answer questions, to help horses that get hung up in a stall or with a front leg over a tie rope, and to keep things tidy.

> **Give honest, sensible answers to the questions people ask at the show, even though you are getting tired of the same questions, over and over again.**

The fanciest stalls I have seen were these permanent stalls for the Carlsberg Brewery horses at the Toronto Royal Winter Fair. This photo was taken in the late 1970s.

Jesse Pareo, age 12, won both the Jr. Driver Team and the Jr. Driver Cart classes at the 1992 Belgian Championship II show in Lexington.

Craig Grange is showing his six of Belgians at the 1992 National Belgian Show. With Craig is his daughter, Krista.

Chapter Ten
Braiding and Decorating

GENERAL

Percheron and Belgian mares are shown at **halter** with loose manes and tied or braided tails. Clydesdale and Shire mares are shown at halter with loose or braided manes and tied or braided tails. Stallions and geldings of all breeds are shown at **halter** with braided manes and tied or braided tails. Clydesdale and Shire stallions may also wear a belly band when shown at halter.

All draft horses are shown in harness with braided manes and tied or braided tails.

Horses with black hooves need to have their hoof walls blackened before entering the ring. Cracks and holes should be filled with wood putty, auto body filler, or an epoxy made for that purpose before blackening. For blackening you can use either a commercially prepared hoof blackener or a spray paint. If you use the paint get a dull black, not the gloss or shiny black paint.

Leave yourself plenty of time to groom and decorate your horse before the class. It is far better to be ready early than to be rushing about and getting excited because you are not ready in time. If it is a harness class you are entering you should know how long it takes you to harness, and start the process in plenty of time.

BRAIDING (ROLLING) THE MANE

You should have practiced braiding the mane at home. The showgrounds, on the day of your class, is neither the time nor the place to learn to braid. If you are not comfortable braiding your horse you can probably get another exhibitor to do it for you, but make these arrangements a day or two ahead of time. It isn't fair to another exhibitor to ask him for help braiding unless he has had time to plan for it.

To braid a mane you will need two 5-foot long strips of stretchy (knit) cloth of contrasting colors sewn together end-to-end, a stool or bench to stand on, and some flowers to go in the finished mane.

Braiding benches take many shapes and forms. Some exhibitors get by without them by sitting on the back of their horse, or by using bales of hay or straw

It is possible to braid (roll) the mane while sitting on the horse's back, but to start you will have to kneel or crawl up the neck to see what you are doing. For most people it is better to stand on a braiding bench.

A braiding bench which folds flat for transport.

to stand on. Neither of these methods is recommended. When sitting on the horse's back you can not get up high enough, or forward enough, to see what you are doing when you start the braid at the bridle path. Standing on bales is OK if the bales are big, tight, and square, but usually the bales are not long enough and are wobbly when standing one on top of another.

Braiding benches are not without their problems either. Taking a wood or metal bench into a slip stall, and then standing on it, can be a harrowing experience if your horse is not used to it. I have indicated several places that sell braiding benches in Appendix II.

Mane braiding is an activity which makes you wish you had another hand (or two). We solved this problem by making it a two-man job. Mary moved and twisted the mane hairs and I kept track of and moved the fabric. It gets a little crowded with two people up on the bench — but if you are compatible it can be thought of as some "quality time" for the two of you as you braid the mane, looking out over the backs of the other horses in the barn and keeping track of how the others are doing.

Mane braiding is hard to learn from reading about it in a book. It is a skill that needs to read about (or watched), then tried on a horse (or pony), then read about (or watched) again, and then tried again. After you do a mane or two you need to do a few more to develop your skill.

OK. Let's do it. Brush out the mane. It should be clean and a comb should pull through it easily. But a slippery mane is harder to braid so it is best to keep Show Sheen or other products like that out of the mane.

Earlene Laursen takes small clumps of mane each time she moves the cloth, resulting in a tight and very neat braid.

Tie the horse so that its head is up and cannot be lowered to the ground. When the horse lowers its head while its mane is braided it will tend to pull out the braids.

Take a small clump of hair at the top of the mane, next to the bridle path, and divide the clump into two equal parts. Lay the strip of cloth across the top of the neck, with one color down one side and the other color down the other side, between the two clumps of hair (Step 1).

Cross the two clumps of hair over the cloth strip (Step 2).

Flip the cloth hanging on the right side of the neck over the top of the crossed hairs and onto the other side of the neck (Step 3).

Flip the cloth hanging on the left side of the neck over the top of the crossed hairs and onto the right side of the neck. This is the cloth originally hanging on the left side, not the one you just flipped over there (Step 4).

Pick up a small section of mane from the horse's neck and add it to the clump you are holding — the clump that is farthest from the poll. Then cross this combined clump and the other clump over the cloth just as you did when you started in step 2 (Step 5).

Tug the two ends of the cloth strip tight and cross them over to the opposite sides of the horse's neck, as you did before in step 3.

Continue on down the neck, adding a small clump of hair from the top of the mane after each crossing of the cloth strips. It is important that you always cross the cloth strips in the same manner, e.g. first the strip hanging down on the right and then the strip on the left over the top of what was the right strip.

Six Steps to Braid a Mane

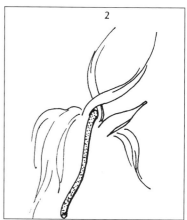

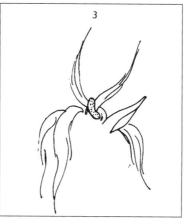

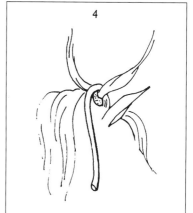

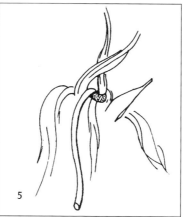

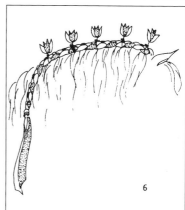

Above are two examples of mane flowers.

When you are coming to the end of the braid you move down the side of the mane for a few more braids and then tie off the remaining ends of the cloth strips into a knot. If the braiding is being done for a hitch class you stop sooner than if it is for a halter class. The braid should not lie under the collar when the horse is harnessed.

After braiding the mane you insert the rosettes or flowers. Typically you would use five flowers when hitching and seven for halter (though some folks use a lot more). The easiest way is to put the first flower in the center of the braided mane, one at each end, and then space the remaining ones in between the end and middle. A flower or rosette usually has a wire at the bottom that can be inserted under the mane roll and then twisted around itself to make it tight and able to stand up straight.

TYING THE TAIL

To tie a docked tail you start by combing out the tail. Then take two large sections of the tail hairs, one from each side, and then comb them out toward the sides. Let the middle section of hairs hang free, as they become the third part of the braid (Step 1 in the illustrations on the next page).

Bring up the middle section of hairs, pulling them tightly across the stump of the bone. Comb them out in an upper motion (Step 2).

Cross the side sections of hairs across the middle section (Step 3). Make this cross as far up the tailbone as you can. This will

Tying the Docked Tail

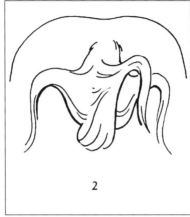

1

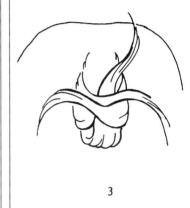

2

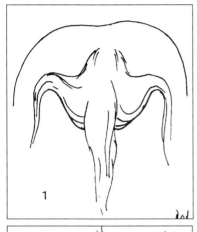

3

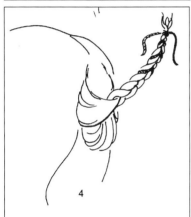

4

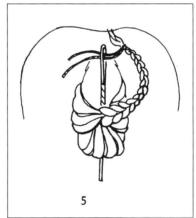

5

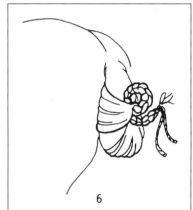

6

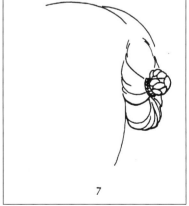

7

determine where the bun will end up. You want the bun as high as possible. Braid normally, preferably in an upward direction (but a downward direction will work).

When you are about five inches from the end of the braid you should incorporate a piece of twine, string, or yarn into the braid. You do this by placing the twine behind the braid, with equal lengths out to both sides, and then picking up these ends along with the two hair clumps out on those sides. The twine is used to tie a knot in the end of the braid (Step 4). The knot is made by making a loop across the braided strand, passing the end of the twin through the loop, and pulling it tight.

Pass a piece of wire bent to form a loop at the end through the knot on the top of the tailbone and insert the end of the braided tail and twine through the loop (Step 5). Pull the end of the tail and twine through the tail hairs and wrap them around

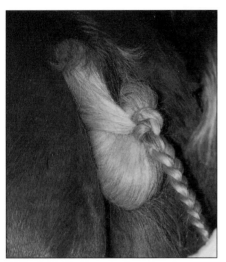

The braided tail after the braid is pulled through the tail hairs to form the knot. It is then wrapped around this knot. Note that the knot is quite far up on the tail bone.

the knot (Step 6). This bunched up area becomes the bun (Step 7). If the tail is especially long you may have to pull the end of the tail up through the bun area with the wire twice.

When you get so that you have just twine going around the tail knot you separate the ends of the twine and go around the knot in opposite directions, finally tying a square knot with the two ends of twine. Cut off the excess twine. If the tail hairs are black you can use liquid shoe polish to dye the twine black. This also helps to set the knot you tied in the twine so it does not come undone.

When you are done tying the tail you will want to place a tail decoration over or around the knot.

Binder twine works well for tying tails, but it might be getting difficult to find. Baler twine is a bit too thick.

BRAIDING THE UNDOCKED TAIL

For many years I have been promoting the idea that we should stop docking the tails of our draft horses. Suffolks are never docked, and many Clydesdales and Shires are not docked. Draft mules never have their tails docked. The practical reasons for this practice are no longer valid, and there are many equally practical reasons (from the horse's point of view) for leaving the tails whole. It has become a cosmetic practice — one which I am sure will eventually disappear.

In several states it is illegal to dock a horse's tail. California, Illinois, and New York are three such states, and there are probably many more. The practice has been illegal in England since 1946. European countries are so adamant on the subject that American Hackney horses with docked tails have recently been denied entrance, even as visitors, to participate in an International driving show.

Many people have told me of their support in this matter, and others have told me I was out in left field (or worse). I do not intend to beat the drum on this subject here, except to say that **you do have a choice.** Think about it before you automatically remove part of your horse's tail.

There may be some judges who believe strongly that tails should be docked, and they might drop a horse with a long tail down in the placings because of it. **That is his/her problem, not yours.** Don't let it become yours.

Tying the Undocked Tail

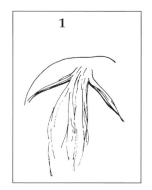

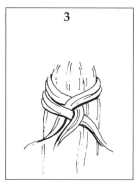
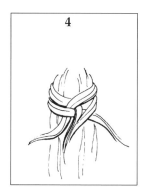

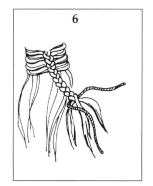
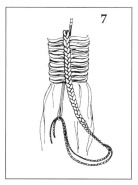

I talked to Ray Bast, longtime president of the Percheron Association about this and his feeling was that a long tail was just fine. If he were judging and the tail covered the legs so he couldn't see the set of the hind leg or the way the hock was built he simply took his cane and pushed the tail to one side.

Actually, you do not have to braid a full tail for the showring at all. Some Clydes and Shires are shown with a full tail, unbraided. Or you might braid some ribbons into the tail, near the top, and have the ribbons hang down alongside the tail hairs. Or you can completely braid the long tail so that it is out of the judge's way to see your horse. The following description and drawings will show and tell you how to braid an undocked tail — as is commonly done to hunters, jumpers and dressage horses when they are shown. Keep in mind that the main reason you are braiding is so that the tail does not cover (hide) the horse's hind legs and hocks.

Pick up two small sections of hair from the top of the tail, one from each side (Step 1). Cross the right section over the left section.

Pick up a small section from the left side of the tail and bring it over the top of the other two sections (Step 2). There now should be three strands for braiding.

Appendix II at
the end of
this book
includes
sources for
decorating
supplies.

Cross the bottom strand over (Step 3). Pick up a new section of hair from the right side of the tail and add it to the strand you just crossed over (Step 4). Cross over the bottom strand (which now is sticking out on the left side of the tail. Add a new section from the left side of the tail and add it to the section you just crossed over (Step 5).

Continue crossing over and adding hairs until you reach the end of the tailbone. Keep a steady pressure and tighten each braid as you cross over. When you reach the end of the tailbone you add the remaining hairs to your strands and continue the braid to the end of the tail.

Near the end of the tail incorporate a piece of string or yarn into the braid (Step 6). This will be used to tie off the end of the braid and to thread the braid up through the tail (Step 7). Tie off the end of the braided tail by making a loop with the string, passing the end of the string through the loop, and pulling tight.

Insert a wire with a loop on its end down through the braid on the tailbone and pull the braid up through itself. Use the ends of the twine to tie it to the tailbone. You can finish by tying bows to the tailbone.

SPRIGS

Sprigs are upstanding decorations placed on either side of the tail, at the very top of the tail. (See the lower left photo on the next page.) They are most often used on Clydes and Shires. To learn more about this added tail decoration I recommend that you get a copy of Marion Young's booklet on Showmanship of Clydesdales (see Appendix II). If you are showing Clydes or Shires you should have this booklet anyway.

Sources for the ribbons, rosettes, bows, and sprigs described in this chapter can also be found in Appendix II at the end of the book.

The photos on the next page show a variety of tail decorations. The top three are undocked tails. The bottom three are docked tails.

Todd Draheim is showing Brass Rings Commander Reno, owned by Locust Grove Clydesdales, to First Place Yearling Futurity Stallion at the 1996 National Clydesdale Show in Milwaukee.

Davey Fry is showing Rex, owned by Tom Brislawn, to Grand Champion Gelding at the 1996 National Clydesdale Show in Milwaukee.

Chapter Eleven
Showing at Halter

GENERAL

Percherons and Belgians are shown at halter with a white show halter. Clydesdales are shown in either a white show halter or a clean rope halter. The white show halters should, in fact, be white. Clean and polish them with white shoe polish when they get dirty. Stallions are shown with a white show bridle with a straight snaffle bit and a lead chain under the chin. If you are showing a mare that is hard to handle you may want to use a bridle on her as well.

You should carry a short (about 18 inches long) show stick in your left hand. The show stick is optional when showing Clydes or Shires. You hold the lead line in your right hand and the show stick in your left.

Make sure your number is securely fastened to the back of your shirt or belt.

Do not enter the showring wearing your everyday or barn clothes. Blue jeans and T shirts are not appropriate for showing at halter. You and your helper or whip person (called a "trailer") should wear outfits that are clean and matching (or at least similar).

When you bring several horses into the ring at the same time, as in the Championship classes or in some of the larger group classes, you may have to ask someone who is not normally involved in showing your horses to hold a horse for you. In these instances it is alright if that person is dressed more casually.

LAST MINUTE GROOMING

We will assume that your horse was bathed (or vacuumed well) the day before, and that any manure spots from last night have been washed out.

You will want to give your horse a good brushing, and

This is E.J.G. Barb, the most celebrated Belgian mare in the 1990s, owned by John Leask and shown here by Don Lowes.

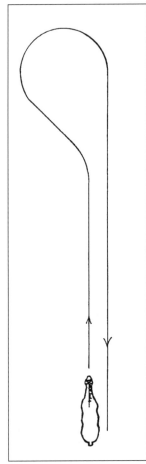

The golf club turn used when showing at halter.

then wipe him off with a rag dampened with a good fly spray, being sure to get the legs and under the belly.

Trim any long hairs about the face and muzzle (except for Clydes) and apply a light coating of baby oil on the muzzle and around the eyes.

Blacken the hooves and do whatever braiding is necessary for the class you are entering.

LINE-UP OF CLASSES

Horses are shown at halter as individuals against other horses of the same age and as members of groups. All horses become a year older, for showing purposes, on January 1. A horse born on December 28 is considered a yearling when it is a week old. A horse is considered to be a foal during the entire calendar year in which it was born. Horses born early in the year have an advantage when shown at halter during their first and second years, but this advantage pretty well disappears by the time they are 3-year-olds.

When entering classes you must go by the rules set forth by the particular show. If there are no specific rules the following general rules usually apply.

Yeld Mares are aged mares who did not raise a foal in the current year. Brood Mares are aged mares that did raise a foal in the current year.

The foal shown in the Mare and Foal class is the foal raised during the current year. Produce of Dam means two animals of any age or sex with the same Dam (mother). Get of Sire means two or three animals of any age or sex with the same Sire (father). There seems to be a growing tendency to reduce the number of horses in the Get of Sire class from three to only two animals, at least in the smaller shows.

Borrowing horses. Generally you can borrow a horse from another exhibitor to make up your (3 animal) Get of Sire, a grand display, and the six horse hitch. Check the rules at the show you are attending, and if it is not covered in the rules you should ask the Show Chairman.

ENTERING THE RING

You should enter the ring at a trot on the left side of the horse and proceed to the end of the line of horses waiting for the judge. **You should start showing your horse the minute you enter the ring, whether or not the judge is watching, and keep showing until**

the judge turns in his placings to the ringman. Make sure you are wearing your exhibitor's number.

WAITING IN THE LINEUP

Stand your horse up properly in the line-up with front legs square on the corners and back legs together — and keep him there. Pay attention to the routine being asked for by the judge. Do not approach the judge when it is your turn without a clue as to what you are to do.

If you are showing a foal or yearling do not stand directly in front of your horse. Young horses get bored easily and, when bored, may strike out or paw with their front feet. You don't want to be in the way when they do this.

SHOWING YOUR HORSE TO THE JUDGE

Smile.

When it is your turn to show keep your horse standing properly in the line-up until the judge looks over and indicates that he is ready for you. Do not be too quick to move out. Give the judge a chance to form a first impression of your horse while he is still in the line-up. On the other hand, don't make the judge wait.

Normally you will lead your horse up to the judge at a walk, then turn him and lead him away. You might be asked to lead him down and back at a walk and then lead down and back at a trot, or you might be asked to lead him down halfway at a walk and then start trotting, and then do the same on the way back. Sometimes the judge will ask the exhibitors to form a circle and walk, and then trot, as he stands in the center of the circle. Understand what he wants, and do it.

You always lead your horse from the horse's left side. When

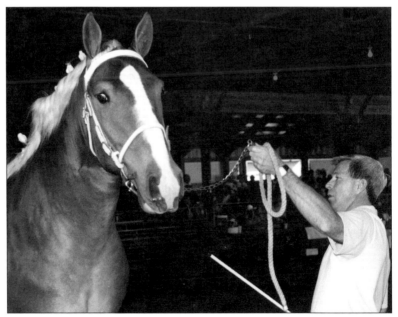

Jack Hale is showing one of his young mares at the National Belgian Show in Davenport, Iowa.

turning at the end to come back toward the judge you take a few steps out to the left and then push your horse around to the right. Make a wide turn so the judge can watch your horse from the side as he turns around. This is sometimes called the "golf club turn." You want to end up your turn so you are facing the judge in about the same place as you were when you started the turn. Remember **you push your horse around the turn** — do not pull him around.

Move in a straight line away from the judge, and then in another straight line back toward the judge. He wants to watch how your horse moves when standing directly behind and directly in front — he can't see how the horse moves when you go off to the side.

Smile.

If you need a trailer (whip person) to help your horse trot he/she should run at least ten feet behind you. Some think the trailer should be on the left side of the horse, but this seems to make some horses trot sideways with their hind ends out to the (right) side. Others think the trailer should be on the right side of the horse, but this may cause the horse to "run over" his handler. So, depending on the tendencies of your horse you should tell the trailer which side he should go on

It is important that the trailer does not block the judge's view of the horse. The trailer should not crack or move the whip unless it is necessary to get the horse to move out. Too often the trailer cracks the whip and gets the horse into a canter or gallop — not at all what was wanted. Canadians seldom use a whip or trailer when showing at halter, and generally will not permit a trailer when they are doing the judging.

While moving your horse you should keep one eye on the horse and the other eye on where you are going. It looks very bad just to run or walk out and not be aware of your horse. Take another look at the picture on the cover of this book and see how Randy is keeping an eye on the judge and on the horse.

Remember to smile when you are showing your horse.

Amber Butler was the winner in the Belgian Showmanship (age 10–15) Class at the 1997 Michigan Great Lakes International.

Your horse should move in a straight line with his head up. He should be animated and look alive. Do not let your horse drag his feet, stumble, or drop his head down. If you are animated and alert chances are your horse will be the same. Some of the best handlers (Corbly Orndorff and Jack Hale immediately come to mind) lean back and pick up their feet high, often in step with the horse. This seems to make the horse more animated — or at least it appears that way. By the same token, if the handler has trouble running himself, or has a limp, it detracts from the way of going of the horse. You should look alive and act like you are enjoying yourself while moving your horse during the halter class. Smile.

After you have moved your horse you stand it up in front of the judge for his or her inspection. The judge will look at the head and then walk around the horse. He will often check the hoof heads on the front feet for sidebones. Keep your horse still and standing properly. He must be kept standing on all four feet, not on three feet with one resting.

This is the time when you may want to practice a little deception. The object is to present your horse in the best possible way, even to the point of deceiving the judge. If your horse tends to be crooked-legged, or sickle hocked, you will want to stretch him a little when you stand him up to hide that tendency. Or if your horse tends to camp out behind (See Chapter 1), then stand him so that his back legs are a little under himself.

The easiest way to stand your horse is to slowly back him until he has his back feet where you want them. Then raise his head and pull him forward, ever so gently, until he sets his front feet where you want them. Then give the lead a gentle tug and tell him to stand. Of course this is something you will have practiced at home before the show.

Never stand your horse up where his hind feet are on higher ground than are his front feet. If there is a higher spot of ground near where you are standing your horse up for the judge you should make sure that his front feet are on that higher spot.

Resist the tendency to stretch your horse, as is done with Saddlebreds and some other riding breeds. But if you have to err, a horse that is stretched a little looks better than one that is standing with his feet too far underneath him.

After the judge is through with examining your horse you should **trot** off to where the horses that have been judged are standing. If the judge liked your horse at all he will watch him again as he trots away and back into the lineup. Be sure to take advantage of this additional opportunity to show off your horse.

You should stand your horse up in front of the judge in a way that emphasizes his strong points and minimizes his defects.

Then stand your horse up again and **keep him standing properly until** all the horses have all been judged and **the judge turns his placings in to the ringman.** A little conversation with your fellow showmen is OK, especially in a large class where there is a lot of waiting for the others to work their horses, but don't lose track of what you are doing out there. If it is a very large class you can let your horse relax a little while you are waiting. Don't be one of those that is constantly jerking on the lead chain. But always be aware of where the judge is, and what he is doing.

Put the ribbon your horses won in the individual classes on their halters when bringing them back for a group class.

GROUP CLASSES

Normally you may **not** show a horse in a group class if it was not shown already as an individual. When you bring your horses back for the group classes you should put the ribbons they won earlier on their halters. If your horses did well as individuals you will want them to wear their ribbons in the group classes. If they didn't do well it is just a courtesy to the judge — his job is hard enough already — to show the ribbons and help him place the groups correctly.

SHOWMANSHIP CLASSES

Showmanship classes are those where the handler is being judged (not the horse) on how well he or she is showing the horse. These classes are intended for younger people, and are helpful in teaching these youngsters the art of showmanship.

The horse used in a showmanship class should be one that can be expected to stand and move properly. Nothing is guaranteed in the showring, but you certainly do not want to give the young person the disadvantage of showing a horse known to be unruly or difficult to show. It is unwise and dangerous, for the same reasons, to use a foal or stallion in a showmanship class.

Megan Hagemann is showing in Junior Showmanship at the 1993 Walworth County (Wisconsin) Fair.

Chapter Twelve
Showing In Harness

GENERAL

There are many books and pamphlets which deal with the proper way to fit a harness to a particular horse, how to hook your horses to the vehicle, and how to string the lines — so we will not deal with that here. Suffice to say, you should fit your harness to the horse **before** arriving at the show. If you use a farm harness at home, and this will be your first experience with a show harness, you will find the many different pieces very confusing.

It takes more helpers to show in harness (than at halter). A good rule of thumb is that you need a helper for each horse you plan to hook (at one time). That is, if you plan to hook a team you need two helpers (besides the driver). If you are going to hook a Unicorn you need three helpers (besides the driver).

> It takes lots of help to hitch. You should figure on one person per horse.

WHAT IS BEING JUDGED

In a harness class the judge is primarily concerned with the way your horse(s) are moving. Lameness is a fatal flaw, as it is in a halter class. The judge will be rewarding horses that move with animation, show good action with both front and back legs, have good head-set, and cover lots of ground. These are big horses, and they should pick up their feet and set them back down with conviction. They should be responsive to the teamster's commands.

If there is more than one horse in the hitch they should work together, in unison, as

Lyn Langston of Quailhurst Farm is showing her Clydesdale unicorn at the 1982 Boone County (Illinois) fair. It is nice to see a wagon that is a little different than the conventional delivery wagons that are ordinarily used. This stake wagon, now owned by Live Oak Plantation, has a fifth wheel and is appropriate for a team, unicorn, and four.

much as possible. The wheel team should pull the wagon, and the tugs on the swing and lead horses should be a little loose. The tugs on the wheel team should never be loose, except when standing or backing.

The judge will probably stand in front of the horses as they come toward him along the rail so he can see if they are picking up their front feet in a straight line, without excessive winging.

At the walk the judge will expect to see a nice flat-footed walk. The horses should not prance or play around when asked to walk.

In the lineup the horses should stand quietly, without excessive head tossing or mouthing of the bit. When asked to back they should be responsive and work together.

Although the main consideration in judging a hitch class is the way in which the horses work, the judge will also consider the turnout itself. Are the horses and harness clean? There is nothing like a little sweat after a few rounds in the ring to bring out any dirt in either the horse or harness. Does the harness fit the horse properly? Is the vehicle appropriate and clean?

The walk is just as important as the trot. Your horse should walk, not prance or jog in place.

BITTING

Most newcomers to draft horses start with a farm harness, where the bridle is equipped with a straight snaffle bit. These people often assume that the straight snaffle is the only way you should drive a draft horse. They then have a runaway or two at home and get discouraged.

When draft horses were really worked in the fields and on the streets they learned to stand — they got tired and wanted to stand and rest. Today we tend to feed our horses better and work them less, and they are more unpredictable.

I was having problems like this, and I happened to mention it to Dr. Lepird while watching him show his Belgians at the Iowa State Fair. He asked me what kind of bit I was using and I told him a straight snaffle. He suggested I switch to a buxton bit with a

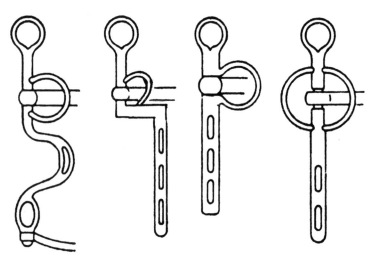

Some curb bits with a shank which you might find on a show bridle. From the left, the Buxton bit, Elbow bit, Gig bit, and Liverpool bit. The further down you attach the lines the more pressure you will put on the horse's mouth and chin.

chain under the chin. I did, and that was the end of any runaways for me.

The only place where you should use a straight snaffle bit is in the farm team class.

Most show bridles come with a buxton, liverpool, or elbow bit where you can attach the lines in several places to achieve more or less leverage under the chin of the horse. These bits also have a ring where the lines can be attached giving no leverage. Do not use this ring. Attach your lines to the bar that extends down and give yourself some advantage in holding back a horse that might want to run, or that might get spooked and start running.

As you move the lines down on the shank you increase the pressure and leverage on the horse's jaw, and you have to be more gentle and sensitive when working the lines. Moving the lines down gives you the opportunity to hold a horse back more, but it also gives you the responsibility to be more sensitive to your horse's mouth. Learn the position that is best for each horse you are driving. They are all different, and sometimes a particular horse will need more leverage one day than he does on another day.

Some horses are driven with a straight snaffle overcheck bit which is separate from the bit in the bridle. This gives more opportunity to get the horse's head up without interfering with the operation of the lines on the bit. The separate overcheck bit is usually fastened back to the harness with straps that go up between the horse's ears and over his poll.

In a hitch class you will often see the helper jump down from the seat and adjust the lines on the bit of one or more horses when they stand in the lineup, or when there is a pause in the action while they are waiting for another entry to come into the ring. These adjustments are made to horses that are pulling too hard (where the helper will move the lines down) and to horses that are dragging behind (where the helper will move the lines up).

If you take a careful look at the hitch pictures in this book you will see all combinations of line placement in the bit. Alan is driving his team with the lines in the snaffle position (shown opposite page 1), as do all of the horses that can be seen in Henry's Argonaut Shire six (page 18). But most of the other hitches use several combinations of line placement, with the first slot down used quite often.

I have seen a lot of runaways in the ring and they usually occur when the lines are attached to the ring on the bit, making the bit work like a straight snaffle. I know that bit leverage will not guarantee that you can stop your horses, but it sure helps. Use it.

Craig Grange (with the lines) and J. W. McKeehan about to enter the ring at the 1979 Wisconsin State Fair. Note their matching outfits, including their bright yellow sport coats. The McKeehan Belgians were an out-standing hitch in the 1970s and early 1980s.

CONFIDENCE

Driving a draft horse should be fun. Do not enter the ring if you are afraid. Don't let anyone else drive your horses if they are afraid. The horses can tell if the teamster is afraid, and they will become afraid (or less confident) as a result.

I have seen many ladies who were scared to death go into a Ladies Cart class. They were entered by their husband just because the class was available and they end up having trouble or a runaway — often with the lines attached to the snaffle ring on the bridle. They did not drive the horse at home, but it was just too hard for the husband or owner to pass up a chance to show in that class. It is for just this reason that the Ladies Cart Class was removed from the schedule at the Michigan Great Lakes International show. (Instead of Ladies Cart they have a cart class for mares, and another for geldings, and both men and women are welcome in either class.)

Showing in a hitch class should be fun. Don't enter the class if you are afraid.

Another example of horses being able to sense the ability and mood of the teamster is when you see a pulling team bolt before they are hooked to the sled, even when there are two or three men holding the lines to prevent this. After two such tries, and with only one more allowed, I have seen a new person take the lines by himself and talk the team up to the sled where they were hooked without any trouble. Horses know if the person holding the lines is scared or nervous. It is OK to be excited before going into the class, but if you are scared or afraid you aren't ready and should scratch the class. Better safe than sorry.

HARNESS CARE

Show harness is very expensive. If you take good care of it it will last your lifetime, and your children's lifetime. But if you don't, it won't.

Harness must be kept clean and well oiled. A good practice is to wipe down the harness pieces completely with a soft, damp cloth each time you remove it from the horse, and before it is put away. Use a mild soap, such as Murphy's soap, in the water to help wash away the sweat and crud that builds up on the harness. Then, when the harness is dry, a light wiping with a good harness conditioner will replenish the oils that were removed by the sweat and soap.

At the end of the show season most exhibitors will keep their show harness in their house, rather than in the barn. The humidity and temperature extremes that you find in the barn are hard on harness.

At least once a year you should completely take apart the harness in order to clean and oil the spots you cannot reach in any other way. We did this job out on the front lawn where there was plenty of room to spread out the parts.

There is no really good way to store and transport harness. Most people end up using harness boxes — one for the harness for each horse. These boxes are often arranged inside so that the harness hangs on hooks and supports when the box is placed on its end. This works alright, but these boxes are very heavy to carry and the harness invariably gets mixed up inside the boxes when they are transported.

> Safety is the most important consideration when showing draft horses in harness.

SAFETY

Everything you do when showing in harness should be done as safely as possible. There are a lot of opportunities for injury, and you should always keep safety in mind.

One rule which is stressed over and over again in driving horse shows held under the rules of the American Driving Society (ADS) is that you must never remove the bridle from your horse while it is still hitched to the vehicle. This also means you should never hitch a horse to the vehicle without

Audrey Bunston drives her gelding, Doug, at the 1991 Britt show. She has good contact with the horse through the lines, is holding her whip with her right hand, and has a smile that just won't quit. She knows what she is doing and enjoys doing it.

having the bridle on. The ADS is so emphatic on this point that if you have an unbridled horse hitched to a vehicle at an ADS show you will be asked to leave the showgrounds immediately.

There is a proper sequence to hitching and unhitching. When hitching you should always harness the horse first, with the lines attached to the bridle and coiled up and draped over the hames. When hitching to a cart have someone stand at the head of the horse and bring the cart to the horse with the shafts held high. Talk to the horse and touch his hindquarters with the shafts to let him know what you are going to do. Bring the shafts down over the horse's back to the proper position and slide them into the shaft carrier loops on the harness. Hook the tugs to the single-tree on the cart and buckle in the back-up straps. Bring the lines back to the seat and drape them over the back of the seat where they will be convenient to grab. The teamster then gets into the seat and when he is ready asks the person at the horse's head to stand aside.

Never remove the bridle until the horse is unhooked from the vehicle.

When hitching a team to a wagon only the outside lines are attached to the bridle when bringing the horses to the wagon. When the horses are in position alongside the pole, with one person at the head of each horse, attach the cross lines to the inside of the bit on each horse. Take the ends of the lines back to the wagon seat and give them to the helper that is on the seat, or, if there is no one on the seat, drape them over the dashboard or seat where they can be reached from the ground. Next hook the neck yoke to the pole with the straps or chains that are provided for that purpose. The last thing to be connected are the tugs to the doubletrees. Never connect the tugs (traces) before the pole. Make sure the tugs cannot disconnect from the doubletrees — tape them with black electrical tape if necessary. Drop enough links on the tug chains so that the neck yoke pulls slightly to the rear when the tugs are tight.

When unhitching you follow the same procedure in reverse. The main points are to have someone at the head of each horse, you always unhook the tugs before unhooking the neck yoke (on a team), and you never

Glen Schrader driving a Tom Miller Belgian gelding at the 1989 Belvidere, Illinois, show.

remove the bridle until the horses are free of the vehicle and back in the stall area.

SHOWING IN CART

Smile.

Most people start their harness showing with the cart. We will not go into all of the details of hooking to the cart, as they are covered by several other books, but there are a few points to remember.

The cart should have an easy way of getting in and out, without having to put your foot in the wheel spokes and climb over the wheel.

Make sure the tugs are secure on the single-tree. If there is a possibility they can come loose then tape them with black electrical tape.

Carry a whip, or have a whip in the whip-holder where it is easy to grab should you need it. In the showring the whip should be in your hand.

Dress appropriately. Remember, this is a show. Men should wear a hat, coat, and tie. Ladies look nice in a dress or skirt and hat.

Attach the exhibitor number to the back of the cart. One way to do this is to tape it to the back of the seat using black electrical tape.

A header is perfectly permissible (even expected) during the lineup for juniors and for lady drivers. Adult men who are in doubt as to whether or not their horse will stand properly in the lineup should also arrange to have a header. These headers need not be dressed as nicely as the driver, but neither should they look as though they just finished cleaning the barn.

SHOWING A TEAM

Smile.

Have someone ride alongside you on the seat. If it will be two men then both should wear matching jackets and hats. Ladies can wear slacks when sitting on the seat of a wagon. The second person will be needed if there is any type of emergency, if the lines get tangled or need to be adjusted on the bit, or as a header in the lineup.

When driving a pair you should also hold the whip in your hand, along with the lines. If you find it difficult to hold the whip when driving more than two horses because of the added number of lines in your hands then make sure the whip is somewhere where you can get it if you need it. Most teamsters put the whip on the seat behind them.

Make sure that the tugs cannot come loose from the eveners on the vehicle. If they are attached with a hook and loop you should tape

The tugs should be fastened securely to the evener. Use black tape if there is a possibility that they can come loose.

them with black electrical tape so they cannot come loose. A large snap clasp is better than a hook and loop.

Photo provided by Jim Richendollar.

The antique hitch (delivery) wagons have a life of their own, and they live on and on. The wagon now being used by Live Oak Plantation was earlier used by Harold Clark of Meadowbrook Farm. Some dimensions on this wagon are: the box is 52" wide x 12' long, the seat is 92" from the ground, the front wheels are 41" in diameter, and the rear wheels are 53" in diameter.

RING PROCEDURES

Give yourself plenty of room when entering the ring. Don't enter too closely behind the exhibitor ahead of you. If the ring is crowded, or if you are behind a slowpoke, you may have a problem in showing your horses. It is not acceptable to pass another hitch in the showring. What you can do when stuck behind a slowpoke is slow your hitch on the side of the ring where the judge is not watching which will give you some room to drive ahead when you get to the side of the ring where the judge is. Another trick is to use the entire ring, driving into the corners as much as you can, which will tend to free up some room in front of you in which to work.

Sit up straight and smile. Everyone, **including the judge,** likes to see the teamster look like he/she is enjoying him/herself. Teamsters generally look better when they keep their legs together rather than sitting with their legs far apart. If you have trouble remembering this you might try crossing your legs at the ankle.

Normally you enter the ring at a trot, moving in a counter-clockwise direction. Of course if the ring steward tells you something different, or if the hitches that entered the ring before you are doing something different, you follow their instructions or lead.

An adult should always ride along with a Junior Driver. This is required by the rules for most shows. If it isn't, it should be.

The placings in a hitch class are often called out in reverse order, leaving the winner alone in the ring at the end of the class. If you are the winner, and if you are asked to make a "victory pass" around the ring before leaving, you should resist the temptation to show off with a figure eight or other fancy maneuver. Horses are often jumpy when they are left alone in the ring at the end of the class and may not perform well for you. Just make your victory pass around the ring and get out.

The fanciest wagon I have ever seen was this one owned by the Carlsberg Brewery, shown here as it was on display at the Toronto Royal Winter Fair.

Doug Palmer is driving the wagon Carlsberg used in the showring — still fancy but not quite as elaborate as the one above.

This shire team, owned by Tom Schwartz (standing) and driven by his son, Tim, are hooked to an English style wagon. The teamster sits in a high seat, with a sign above his head, and the groom or assistant driver stands in the box behind the driver.

Near and Off, Gee and Haw

Two sets of words often used when driving horses are *Near & Off* and *Gee & Haw*.

Near and *Off* refer to the side of the horse or the team, with *Near* being the left side and *Off* being the right side. It is thought that right-handed men usually their wore swords on their left side, and that it was therefore easier for them to mount their horse from the left side — less interference when lifting the leg over the horse's back. As the rider was most often on the left side of his mount, this became known as the *Near* side, with the right side becoming the *Off* side.

The way I remember which is which is that when driving a team down the road, the right-hand horse is the one in danger of falling *Off* the side of the roadway.

Gee is a verbal command for a right turn, and *Haw* is a verbal command for a left turn. Don't ask why — it just is.

Chapter Thirteen
Show Photos & Photographers

Just as I have a soft spot in my heart for draft horse farriers and judges, I also have one for horse show photographers.

Being a photographer at a horse show is not an easy job, and draft horse shows are among the hardest. I enjoy taking pictures for my own use at a horse show, but it becomes work when you are the official photographer and expected to photograph everybody. When I do it, it's because I enjoy it.

If draft horse people don't start to do a better job of supporting the photographers working at their shows there soon will be no photographers that will take these jobs. It already is getting hard to get competent people for some of the bigger shows, and several Midwestern state fairs have just given up. I have never made a profit being the official photographer at a draft horse show.

It is natural to hold off buying pictures until the end of the show season. After all, you might get a better one at the next show. So you wait, and then in October you realize that you need a photo for an ad in the *Draft Horse Journal*, or for the All-American competition, so you make a frantic call to a photographer and try to get a print, RUSH. That's not fair, and it won't work — either for you or for the photographer.

Support the photographer working your show. Buy a print or two (or more), even if you aren't sure you will need them. The amount you spend for pictures will be just a fraction of what you spent getting to the show and while you were there, and the pictures will be a tangible reminder of the experience. You will be glad you have the photos later.

You might also find that a picture or two will give you an insight as to what you are doing wrong, or right, in the showring. After all, we all look different than we think we do and a picture is one way of seeing how we look to other people.

While I am on my soapbox let me add that I think the show chairman has the responsibility to see that the photographer's presence does not detract from the overall appearance of the show. It makes no sense to ask the exhibitors, judge, and ring people to dress properly and then let a photographer who is not dressed properly into the center of the ring.

Proper dress for a show photographer consists of more than some cameras around your neck. This lady was in the ring at the Wisconsin State Fair.

Marion Young after winning the Ladies' Cart at the 1991 National Clydesdale Show in Milwaukee driving Joker.

Pete Lippitt and his daughter, Pam, at the 1980 Waterloo (Iowa) Dairy Cattle Congress.

Chapter Fourteen
Between Shows

If you have some time at home between shows you should check the horses' shoes, and tighten those that are loose. If the feet are getting too long you should have them reset.

You will want to keep them inside during the hot summer days so that their coats do not become dull and faded, and so they don't throw a shoe while stomping at flies. Shoes thrown in a pasture are very difficult to find. They seem to blend in with the grass within minutes.

If the next show is several weeks away (or longer) you will want to work your horses just like you did before the show season started, practice haltering your halter horses and hitching your harness horses.

If the harness was not cleaned thoroughly after the last hitch class at the last show it should be cleaned while you are at home, before going to the next show.

A notebook with a page for each show, with comments about the show and the placings you got, will be very helpful later.

You will want to keep a little notebook where you keep track of which horses you showed at which shows, and how they placed. It is important that you make this record as you go through the show season as it is very easy to forget who did what, where, after the season is over. This notebook will become very useful when selling horses, writing ads about your horses, and deciding which horses to show next year.

Mike Deneen is showing his Belgian Gelding at the 1996 Walworth County (Wisconsin) Fair.

Chapter Fifteen
The End of the Show Season

The show season used to have a definite beginning and end. Now it seems to go on continuously, all year long. At least it can if you want it to.

But for most beginners you will decide to stop showing in the fall, perhaps after your county or state fair.

Make sure you trim your horses' hooves back when you remove their shoes at the end of the show season.

You should pull the shoes and trim the feet of your show horses before putting them out to pasture. Sometimes you will have to stay at the last show for a day or so before being released, and you will remove the shoes then, before the trip home. It is important that the hooves be trimmed back to remove the excess hoof wall that has grown out while the horse was shod for the show.

When you do turn them out to pasture remember that they have been eating hay while at the shows, and are not used to pasture. If your pasture is lush and rich you will want to let them out gradually, starting with a only a few hours at first, until they get used to the change in diet. If your pasture is dry and burned out then this is not a problem.

Give your harness one last good cleaning and hang it up where it will not be exposed to dust and extremes of temperature and humidity. A spot in the basement will do, or in an upstairs closet.

Make some final notes in the notebook you are keeping of the show results for the past year.

Daren Fischer driving six Percherons before a packed grandstand at the 1997 Walworth County (Wisconsin) Fair.

Chapter Sixteen
Harness, Carts, and Hitch Wagons

There are many harness makers throughout North America. To find one in your area you can ask someone, check the ads in one of the draft horse magazines, or purchase a copy of one or both of the two directories designed to help you find draft horse suppliers, *The Reach* and *The Evener*. Information about the magazines can be found at the end of this book in Appendix I, and the directories can be purchased from the Mischka Farm bookstore.

Used carts and hitch wagons can be purchased at many of the draft horse auctions held throughout the year. These auctions are advertised in the draft horse publications.

There are many shops that manufacture new carts and hitch wagons. There are probably a dozen cart manufacturers in northern Indiana alone. It would not make sense for me to try to list them all. But in Appendix V I have listed three cart sources from widely different parts of the country as a place to start. *The Reach* and/or *The Evener* are again useful in finding these shops. Or you could look on the back of a wagon or cart that you see and admire at a show to see if the manufacturer has attached a name plate. If you don't find a nameplate just ask the owner about his vehicle — he will be happy to tell you about it.

Another option is to build your own vehicle. If you want to build a cart you might buy the wheels, axle, springs, and shafts and then go ahead and build the seat. For a wagon you might buy the running gear (wheels, axles, fifth wheel, springs, and pole) and build the box and seat.

On the following pages there are pictures of some of the carts and wagons in use today.

A Phaeton draft cart manufactured by Olson Carriage and Harness.

This photo illustrates the proper way to hitch the horse to a cart. The tugs go between the billet or belly-band and the shaft loop. The shaft loop goes around the shaft and then buckles down into the outer girth. The hold-back strap goes from the breeching to a metal loop on the shaft. This particular cart has an extra strap going from the collar to a hook on the top of the shaft that would come into play if the tug were to come loose from the single-tree.

A split-seat rear entry draft horse show cart.

A Meadowbrook style rear-entry cart manufactured by Olson Carriage.

A delivery wagon with a stake box built by Olson Carriage and Harness.

A light delivery wagon suitable for a team.

A handsome wagon owned by Windermere Farms of Spring Mills, Pennsylvania.

Wagons with automobile tires are frequently towed behind a truck like a trailer, especially by Canadian exhibitors.

Four views of the Rocking Horse Ranch wagon, one of my favorites.

The wagon owned by Rice's Percherons is not painted — it is natural wood.

Chapter Seventeen
Parades, Sleigh Rallys and Field Days

I want to end this book sort of where I started, with a reminder that parades, sleigh rallys, and field days are also shows. If you attend these types of events your horses should be clean, well-behaved, and in good condition; your harness should be clean and appropriate to the event; and your clothes should be clean and appropriate as well.

SAFETY

Accidents are best avoided. That said, accidents can and do happen. Safety, especially for the spectators, is extremely important at events of this type. At most shows you and your horses are separated from the spectators by a fence, rail, or ring barrier. But at these parades, rallys, and field days there is no separation, and spectators can often go right up to the horses, creating a potentially dangerous situation.

In today's litigious society we have to be concerned with things like liability insurance. Be sure your liability insurance covers you for any injury or damage caused by either you or your horses when they away from home at a horse event. It also is wise to make sure the sponsoring organization has liability insurance that covers the participants as well as the sponsor.

Your horses should be accustomed to the sights, noises and general commotion that accompanies these events. This is kind of a "chicken and egg" situation. It's hard to get them accustomed to these situations without a "first time", and they will be new to the situation that first time.

One way to alleviate this problem when you are hitching several horses is to have only one of them be new to the situation,

You should remove halters when bridling your horse at a public event. It looks bad to have a halter under the bridle. If you need to tie your horse later for lunch you should put the halters back on — it is unsafe to tie your horse with the rope attached to the bridle.

with the rest of them seasoned veterans. This will reduce your chances for an accident. Have plenty of people on hand to help — people who know what to do around horses. And if a spectator is doing something dangerous (like pushing their stroller in front of your team) don't hesitate to ask them to move back, and then explain the potential danger of their situation.

PARADES

Showing involves a lot of "hurrying up and waiting", and with parades that seems especially true. When you are waiting for your turn (the horses are often at the end in a mixed parade) just consider it an opportunity to spend some quality time with your horses, teaching them to stand. Horses need to learn to stand, and with our busy schedules it is hard to find time to teach them that skill.

It goes without saying that your horses should be clean and well groomed. But, I am sorry to say, it needs to be repeated. One year I drove down to Chicago to see their Christmas parade. I thought it would be a picture opportunity. There was but one hitch of draft horses in the parade, and they were thin greys with gobs of manure hanging on their hips and back legs. Not a pretty sight. I saved money on film that day.

When you enter the parade give yourself plenty of room behind the unit ahead of you. Parades tend to bog down and start. Seldom do they speed up. You cannot show your horses properly if they have their noses in the wagon or float in front of you. With ample spacing you will give the spectators a chance to see you as you approach them, and get a good look at your horses as they go by. If you have some space in front you also have a chance to avoid a halt in the middle of a hill.

Parades often have an ending point where the units disband and then make their own way back to the start where the vehicles are parked. Don't be too quick to strip off your parade clothes or have your outwalkers hop on the wagon. Instead you should consider the trip back to the starting point as another parade, maintaining your

Dean and Keith Woodbury with their six Belgian Geldings in the 1996 Great Milwaukee Circus Parade.

proper dress and outwalkers until you get back to the trailers and unhitch. I always enjoy watching Paul Sparrow take the 40 horse hitch back to the showgrounds at the end of the Great Milwaukee Circus Parade. The official parade might be over, but Paul, his horses and outriders, and the musicians riding on the bandwagon all continue showing until they are back at the barn. And the people watching show their appreciation with applause.

Be aware of the spectators during the parade. Wave to them and they will respond. Acknowledge their applause, and you'll get more. A quiet parade is deadly. Throwing candy is dangerous and should be stopped.

FIELD DAYS

Field days are shows where you and your horses perform in work clothes. These are wonderful events which give the spectators an opportunity to see the horses "close-up and personal" as they do their work in the field.

I like to see clean work harness on the horses at a field day. Patent leather and Scotch collars are not appropriate here.

Safety is again of prime importance. At a show the spectators are confined to specific areas. At parades they are on either side of the street. But at a field day they are literally everywhere — and it is important to keep them from getting hurt.

One summer I saw a runaway at three different field days: sulky plows tipping over or tossing their riders in the air when the plows hit a stone; worn out eveners snapping and the horses pulling the teamster off his seat; horses pulling a wagon full of spectators that become spooked and run off, spilling the passengers out the end of the wagon; and horses breaking the ropes that tie them to their trailer and running into a crowd. These are scary situations. Be safe.

Walt Becker is plowing at the 1997 Fall Field Day sponsored by the Wisconsin Draft Horse & Mule Association.

Postscript

The author would like to know of any additions, corrections, deletions, or changes that the reader thinks should be made in this book so that it would be more useful to the beginner draft horse showman. These changes would be considered for later editions.

Please send your comments to Bob Mischka, N8246 Esterly Road, Whitewater, WI 53190.

Bibliography

Adams, O. R., *Lameness in Horses*, Lea & Febiger, 1966.

Craig, John A., *Judging Live Stock*, The Kenyon Printing & Mfg Co, 1901.

Fell, Alex, *The Complete Book of In-Hand Showing*, J. A. Allen & Co, 1996.

Hale, Jack, *Giving Something Back, Draft Horse Journal*, Autumn 1990 and Winter, 1990/1991.

Hawkins Guide, *Horse Trailering on the Road*, Bluegreen Publishing, 1993.

Kays, D. J., *The Horse, Judging Breeding Feeding Management Selling*, A. S. Barnes & Co, 1953.

Myers, Kristin K., *Draft Horse*, Ohio State University, 1985.

Percheron Horse Association of America, *How to Select Percherons*, Chicago, Ill. 1936, Rev. 1986.

Rayner, Nick & Chivers, Keith, *The Heavy Horse Manual*, David and Charles, 1981.

Rooney, James R., *The Lame Horse, Causes Symptoms and Treatment*, A. S. Barnes & Co, 1974.

So You Want to Show Draft Horses, Draft Horse Journal, 1988.

Straiton, E. C., *The Horse Owner's Vet Book*, J. B. Lippincott Co, 1973.

Strickland, Charlene, *Show Grooming, The Look of a Winner*, Breakthrough Publications, 1995.

Young, Marion, *A Beginner's Guide to Basic Conformation and Judging of Clydesdales*.

Young, Marion, *A Beginner's Guide to Basic Show Preparation and Showmanship of Clydesdales*.

Appendix I
Sources for Additional Information

Mischka Farm Bookstore
N8246 Esterly Road
Whitewater WI 53190
Phone (414) 473 5595
24 hour fax (414) 473 4555
Draft horse books, videos, and calendars. **Free catalog available**

> Each of the books and videos referred to in the text of this book are available from the Mischka Farm Bookstore.

Draft Horse Journal
P O Box 670
Waverly, IA 50677
Phone (319) 352 4046
Fax (319) 352 2232
A quarterly magazine. An essential source of information on upcoming shows, show results, and sources for show supplies.

Small Farmer's Journal
P O Box 1627
Sisters, OR 97759
Phone (541) 549 2064
A quarterly magazine. Includes advertisements for harness makers and vehicles, particularly in the western United States.

Rural Heritage
281 Dean Ridge Lane
Gainesboro, TN 38562
Phone (931) 268 0655
A bi-monthly magazine. Includes advertisements for harness makers and vehicles.

Driving Digest
2533 N Carson St, Suite 2990
Carson City, NV 89706
Phone (702) 841 3768
A bi-monthly magazine devoted to all types of driving, including draft horses. A good calendar of coming events (shows).

Driving West Magazine
P O Box 3133
Paso Robles, CA 93447
Phone (805) 237 8476
Fax (805) 237 9308
A bi-monthly magazine. Particularly useful for light-horse driving people, with a west coast advertising emphasis.

Continued on the next page

Appendix I (Continued)
Sources for Additional Information

The American Driving Society
P O Box 160
Metamora, MI 48455
(810) 664 8666
An organization devoted to the promotion of driving horses in America.

Belgian Draft Horse Corporation of America
P O Box 335
Wabash, IN 46992
(219) 563 3205

Percheron Horse Association of America
P O Box 141
Fredericktown OH 43019
(614) 694 3602

Clydesdale Breeders Association
17346 Kelley Rd
Pecatonica IL 61063
(815) 247 8780

American Shire Horse Association
c/o Sharon McLin
35380 County Road 31
Davis CA 95616
(916) 757 2742

Appendix II
Sources for Show Supplies

Meader Supply
23 Meaderboro Rd
Rochester, NH 03867
Phone 1-800-446-7737
24 hr fax (603) 332 2775
A complete source for draft horse show supplies. A free catalog available.

Taborton Draft Supply
54 Taborton Road
Averill Park, NY 12018
Phone (518) 794 8287
A complete source for draft horse show supplies. A free catalog available.

"Showtime" Draft Horse Show Equipment
815 N Van Buren St
Shipshewana IN 46565
Phone (219) 768 7707
Fax (219) 768 7704
Trailers, blankets, coolers, sweats, tack trunks, braiding benches, grooming supplies, harness supplies.

Permanent Impressions
8713 Jacksontown Rd
Newark OH 43056
Phone (614) 522 6971
Fax (614) 323 4408
A complete source for draft horse show supplies. A catalog available for a nominal fee.

Will Lent Horseshoe Company
5800 W Woodrow Road
Shelby MI 49455
Phone (616) 861 5033
Draft horse shoes and shoeing supplies. A free catalog is available.

Anvil Brand Shoe Co
P O Box 198
Lexington IL 61753
Phone (309) 365 8270
Fax (309) 365 3341
Draft horse shoes and shoeing supplies. A free catalog is available.

Continued on the next page

Appendix II (Continued)

Dianne Brown
73495 120th St
Zearing, IA 50278
Phone 1-800-362-8366
Draft Horse decorating supplies — flowers, mane rolls, tail decorations, sprigs.

Dana Neilson
5601 Beeler Road East
Merritt, MI 49667
(616) 328 4523
Draft Horse decorating supplies — flowers, mane rolls, tail decorations, sprigs. Catalog available.

A Beginner's Guide to Basic Show Preparation and Showmanship of Clydesdales and *A Beginner's Guide to Basic Conformation and Judging of Clydesdales* can be obtained from
Marion Young
RR 3
Listowel, Ont N4W 3G8
Canada
(519) 291 2049
or
Clydesdale Breeders of United States
17346 Kelley Rd
Pecatonica, IL 61063
(815) 247 8780

Appendix III
Horse Show Checklist

WASHING
Hose
Sweat Scraper
Hose End and Shut-off
Shampoo
Show Sheen

FEED AND BEDDING
Grain
Beet Pulp
Hay - 3/4 bale/horse/day
Straw
Shavings - 1 bag/horse
Haybags

SHOWING
Show Halters and Bridles
Harness, incl. bridles and collars
Cart
Wagon
Whips, for halter & driving
Show clothes, incl. hat
Hoof black or paint
Mane braid clothes and flowers
Tail bows
Baby Oil
Sandpaper
Plastic Wood and Body Filler
Braiding bench

WORK CLOTHES & SHAVING STUFF

DECORATIONS
Lumber
Sheets and Bedspreads
Valence
Stall (name) signs
Picture board
Farm sign
Rug for Tack stall

MISCELLANEOUS
Lawn Chairs
Sleeping bags
Cots & Pillows
Rags
Card Table
Refrigerator
Yellow Table
Black electrical tape
Hammer, nails, pliers
Shoeing tools
Fans
Extension cords
Insecticide & hand sprayers
Lead ropes
Tie chains
Show Entry Book
Health papers, incl. coggins
Brushes
Money
Leather punch
Mane comb
Long cotton rope
Clasps for buckets
Buckets
Pop, cooler, & ice
Flashlight
Ladder
Camera & film
Staple gun and staples
Manure cart or wheelbarrow
Pitchfork, broom, shovel
Vacuum
Horse thermometer
Spare tires
Hydraulic jack & tire wrench
Farm checks

Appendix IV
All-American Contest and Shows

The *Draft Horse Journal* and the Belgian, Percheron, and Clydesdale breed associations sponsor a contest each year called the All-American. In general how this works is that pictures of horses that are winners (or place well) at certain specified shows are sent to a panel of judges at the end of the year. These judges pick out the best from these pictures as All-American winners.

This is an attempt to get a consensus winner for the entire country for each age and sex for each breed. There are some problems, since unless the judges actually have seen the horses nominated it becomes a picture contest, and pictures can lie. But it seems to be working, and it gives one more thing for the breeders to use when bragging about their horses.

For the detailed rules of this contest you should consult the *Draft Horse Journal* and your specific breed association.

The shows included in the All-American contest for 1998 are:

National Belgian Show, Davenport, Iowa
Ohio State Fair, Columbus, Ohio
Indiana State Fair, Indianapolis, Indiana
Michigan Great Lakes International, Lansing, MI
Wisconsin State Fair, Milwaukee, Wisconsin
Illinois State Fair, Springfield, Illinois
Iowa State Fair, Des Moines, Iowa
Michigan State Fair, Detroit, Michigan
Minnesota State Fair, St Paul, Minnesota
New York State Fair, Syracuse, New York
National Western Stock Show, Denver, Colorado
Keystone International, Harrisburg, Penn
North American Livestock Show, Louisville, KY
Missouri State Fair, Sedalia, Missouri
North Dakota State Fair, Minot, North Dakota
New England Show, Skowhegan, Maine
South Dakota State Fair, Huron, South Dakota
Nebraska State Fair, Lincoln, Nebraska
Colorado State Fair, Pueblo, Colorado
Washington Extravaganza, Monroe, Washington
Oregon State Fair, Salem, Oregon

Idaho State Draft Horse Show, Sandpoint, ID
Georgia National Fair, Perry, Georgia
Vermont State Belgian Show, New Haven, VT
Mississippi State Fair, Jackson, Mississippi
Minnesota Percheron Show, Rochester, Minn
Virginia State Fair, Richmond, Virginia
Los Angeles County Fair, Pomona, Calif.
Dixie Classic Fair, Winston-Salem, N.C.
Maryland State Fair, Timonium, Maryland
Evergreen State Fair, Monroe, Washington
Boone County Fair, Belvidere, Illinois
Weber County Fair, Ogden, Utah
National Clyde Sale Show, Springfield, Ill.
Michigan Draft Horse Show, Mason, MI
Olmstead County Fair, Rochester, Minn
Eastern Idaho State Fair, Blackfoot, Idaho
Florida State Fair, Tampa, Florida
Fort Worth Stock Show, Fort Worth, Texas
North Idaho International, Sandpoint, Idaho
Addison County Show, New Haven, VT

This show listing is given primarily as a place for exhibitors to go to see a show and to meet other exhibitors. Some of the shows are for all three breeds, and some are just for one or two of the breeds. For the specific rules of the All-American Contest please see the *Draft Horse Journal* and your breed association.

Appendix V
Cart and Hitch Wagons

As mentioned in the text of this book, there are just too many manufacturers and sellers of horse-drawn vehicles to try to list them. The following sources, located in widely separate parts of the country, are given as examples or places you might start:

Meader Supply
23 Meaderboro Rd
Rochester NH 03867
(800) 446 7737
Fax (603) 332 2775
Three styles of carts suitable for draft horses are described in their free catalog.

Troyer Carriage Company
P O Box 116
North Village on State Road 5 North
Shipshewana IN 46565
(219) 768 7135
They manufacture a draft horse show cart, and sell a Meadowbrook cart suitable for draft horses.

Olson Carriage and Harness
10855 Hodgen Rd
Black Forest CO 80908
(719) 495 4486
Manufacturer of show carts and hitch wagons.

Appendix VI
Specific Rules for Showing Shires

There are some differences to be observed when showing Shires as opposed to showing other breeds. The following are some general standards recommended by the American Shire Horse Association. Of course, many of the standards set forth below apply to other breeds as well.

1. The horse must be clean and well-groomed. The horse must be "fit", neither too heavy or too thin.

2. Tails should be braided or put up in some manner so there is no untied hair, so the judge can observe the rear of the horse. Scotch knots are traditional for docked tails, and french braids and/or scotch knots for long tails. Manes should be rolled on stallions and geldings over 1 year of age for halter classes. Braiding manes on mares or foals is optional — it is done in Canada and England. All horses' manes are rolled for hitch classes. Treatment of forelocks is optional, but generally they are not shaved for the showring.

3. Stallion girths (rollers) are encouraged on stallions over 2 years of age. Shires are traditionally shown in russet or black show bridles, but other colors may be used. Mares and foals are shown in white rope halters in England, but you don't have as much control. At county fairs a clean halter and matching leadline is adequate. Use of show sticks or crops is a matter of regional or personal preference.

4. A balanced foot that enhances proper movement is encouraged. Overshoeing is discouraged. Horses under 2 years need not be shod but older horses should be shod. Clear hoof dressing may be used but hooves should not be blacked.

5. Ears and chin may be neatly trimmed. Any hair that sticks out when you fold the ear lengthwise in half should be removed. A bridle path may be trimmed. Further trimming to enhance appearance is permissible.

6. Where mares and foals can be in the showring together the foals should be on a lead with a separate handler.

7. Handlers should be clean and well-groomed. At regional or national shows men should wear slacks and a sport coat and tie. At smaller shows attire may be less formal but should be clean and tidy. Having all handlers from a farm dressed alike enhances the overall presentation.

8. Handlers must be able to make the horse behave. Training should be done at home, not in the showring. Stallions must be shown by competent handlers who are over 18 years of age.

9. The stall and barn areas should be kept clean and tidy at all times. Manure and soiled bedding should be removed promptly.

11. When driving a cart or hitch **Men** at larger shows should wear a suit or sport coat and tie. Hats and gloves are recommended. A whip should be carried for single and team classes. At smaller shows attire may be less formal but the driver and rider should always be clean and tidy.

12. When driving a cart or hitch **Women** may wear a pants suit or blazer and slacks in all but the Ladies Cart Class. In the cart class dressier clothes are generally worn. Hats are sometimes required and always look well. Gloves should be worn and a whip must be carried. Shoes and boots that compliment the outfit should be worn.

Appendix VII
Shire Horse Society Guidelines on Correct Shoeing

The following drawings and comments are taken from the American Shire Horse Association Newsletter of Spring, 1995, and again in Winter 1997.

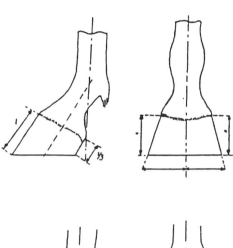

Well Balanced Foot

The correctly trimmed foot should allow frog pressure. This facilitates the absorption and distribution of concussion thus minimizing fatigue and wear to bones, joints and ligaments.

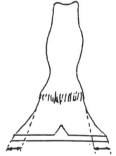

Well Shod Foot

1. The shoe should provide good cover, especially at the heels for support.
2. The clips should be broad and not terminated in a sharp point. The base and height of the clip should be relative to the width of the shoe.
3. Clenches should be of even height, a third of the way up the wall.
4. Beveling should follow the contour of the wall. excessive beveling can lead to injury, e.g. treads, brushing, and resulting Ringbone.

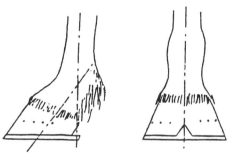

Overlong Feet (Flared or Bell Shaped) or Unbalanced Shoes

Can lead to:
1. Tearing of the lamina of the wall of the hoof from the sensitive laminae covering the pedal bone.
2. Excessive wear on joints and bones resulting in Ringbone or Sidebone.
3. Excessive strain and wear on the flexor tendons.
4. Spavins may form as the result of hind shoes fitted with a single calkin.

For more information about shoeing draft horses the author recommends an article which appeared originally in the *Breeder's Gazette* on August 21, 1912, and was reprinted in the Autumn, 1997 *Draft Horse Journal*, entitled "The Horse's Foot — A Firm Foundation". After the Draft Horse Journal reprint there are comments by two well-known, contemporary horsemen.

The "Last Word"

The following comments from a draft horse judge in England are taken from the book *The Complete Book of In-Hand Showing*, by Alex Fell, published in 1996 by J. A. Allen & Co, Ltd, 1 Lower Grosvenor Place, Buckingham Palace Rd, London SW1W 0EL, England, and are re-printed here with their permission.

"In-hand showing is a waste of time and should be forbidden — function is the only test of a horse!

"One of the blessings of judging a mixed class of heavy horses is that you can only judge what is in front of you, you can't judge what isn't there! With the breed standards fresh in your mind you still, unfortunately, see the way they are shown. If the horse is towing the handler all over the place and not doing what you ask them to do, turning the wrong way, not trotting where they are told and so on, it influences their ranking in order of merit, because you can't compare like with like. Mixed classes are difficult to judge and disheartening to compete in because judges have a natural preference for their own breed. Large classes are difficult to judge too. If you are given twenty mares to judge in forty minutes there is not much time to consider the essentials of feet, limbs, eyes and heights. When I am judging brood mares they have to look as if they are capable of breeding, including width across the pelvis, and have the ability to be a mother, which is expressed in their behavior, as well as pure show points. This doesn't vary much between breeds.

"With regard to conformation, the most fundamental feature is the feet. No foot — no horse. This is followed by the limbs, just like any other horse. Heavy horses have to have a deep chest for work, a good shoulder for the collar, and strong quarters to push them along, which are helped by the weight of the horse. The heavier they are the more pulling power when they lean forward. A Shire can weigh between 17 and 23 cwt.

"The feet should have good hard horn, which has to be blue in the case of the Percheron. For all of them there should be no cracks, or rings which might suggest nutritional or management problems. Sidebones don't bother me because heavy horses have not done any work for years. In a middle-aged horse the lateral cartilages may have ossified a bit, but providing they are still moving well they will have some merit over a spindly object with no bone.

"They should be properly shod and the shoes must not be excessively large. For showing they can be quite exaggerated but they are only show shoes. Nobody would consider working in them. A feature of show shoes, particularly for the Shire and Clydesdale, is beveling, which continues the angle of the wall of the hoof to make the foot appear enormous. Suffolks and Percherons do this to a lesser extent because they have a neater foot. In North America they use what they call a Scotch shoe, which is about a foot square and the sides of the hoof are built up with car body filler to correct and exaggerate the action of the foot. They believe they have to do this to win, but special show shoes don't impress me.

"Another feature of showing in North America is that the horses are very tall. Percherons in France fall into two height ranges: up to 16.2 hh and 16.2 hh and above. In North America they are between 17.2 and 18 hands, so that they are tall and fast for four, six and eight horse turnouts, but they would not be capable of pulling a ten-ton tree trunk...."

"I look for flowing action where the horse covers the ground, rather than high flexion which is so uneconomic of energy and has the horse bashing its feet into the ground. The whole horse must move, not just part of the limbs. A bit of dishing is all right, but not close action. I personally like to see the hocks separated but the Clydesdale people believe that close hocks give better pulling power. In the old days, of course, the working horses were never trotted. They wanted their goods carried and the horse to last for years. Over the years the purpose of working horses has evolved and so has their conformation. I think that their characteristics have to be preserved in a form that could work, even if they do not work very much nowadays...."

"Character is extremely important. Stupidity and uncontrollability get marked down because they are not conducive to work. Handlers need to know what they are doing, not hanging on to the head and preventing the horse from trotting out.They should be level with the horse's shoulder and moving with it. A small handler makes a horse look bigger. They should be well turned out themselves and, ideally, carry a stick because it gives you so much more control. Sticks do not have to be long, although some are, and they help with turning the horse...."

"Feathers must not be whitened artificially so chalk is not allowed. Wood flour is used instead, which is very fine sawdust. Some people clip the docks of Shires and Clydesdales which I cannot say enough against, for the same reasons that docking has been against the law since 1946. There is nothing that this achieves that cannot be achieved by plaiting (braiding) the tail up.

"As I judge a class I think to myself which ones would I like to take home...."

Index of Exhibitors